Testimonial

"Michael has had a truly transformative and immediate impact on how I perform as a leader in the workplace. This has not only helped me focus on how I can maximise my potential as a leader, but also helped me make improvements in every aspect of my life. His coaching has served as an inspiration for me."

~ **Kevin Barrett**, Head of Corporate Development, Sainsbury's Supermarkets Ltd

"Michael has the ability to bring complex ideas across to his audience with coherence, pragmatism and immediate application. I strongly recommend him for developing and delivering instructional programs, executive coaching and professional speaking."

~ **Alexandria Hilton**, Principal, EUROUS Global Executive Development

"Like a lot of owner/managers I had the drive to grow my business but in order to take it to the next level it was crucial that I found out how to improve the balance in my life whilst still leading my company to success. I felt the benefit of our coaching quickly and deeply, and the benefits have lasted."

~ **Neil Ouzman**, Managing Director, OzMO Entertainment Ltd

"Every so often something or someone comes along which challenges your thinking and makes you approach life in a different way. Michael is one of those people. His thoughts, ideas, stories, experience, and especially his use of powerful questions, gave me more than I ever expected and improved my performance more than I could have imagined."

~ **Martin Jones**, Head of Region, South London & Southern Counties, Marks and Spencer

"One of the key learnings for me has been around the support you have given me as a "new boy". Whilst I have been coached before, the focus you were able to put on the first few weeks and days really helped me understand the people, culture and what's expected."

~ **Jonathan Hewett**, Group Financial Services Director, DSGI plc

"Michael will challenge your thinking, stretch your sense of possibility, help you to lead yourself through your own pain barriers and enable you to be a better you…"

~ **Sue Round**, Head of Leadership Development, Sainsbury's Supermarkets Ltd

"As the owner of a small company it is very easy to become lost in the daily detail of running the business, and it can be hard to find high quality advice. I greatly appreciated the clarity and focus that I gained from our calls, through which you helped me a great deal."

~ **Chris Ball**, Managing Director, SMT Network Solutions Ltd

"From the moment Michael walks onto a stage you know that as a corporate presenter and educator he is at the top of his game. Thanks to him my results have amplified considerably and far exceeded my expectations."

~ **Martin Vidakovic**, Director, Lifetime Achievements, Australia

"Before my coaching with Michael I used to move from one aspiration to the next. As a direct result of our work together I feel much more confident, consistently deliver higher quality work, get on better with other people, have clearer goals and, most importantly, I am enjoying the journey."

~ **Jonathan Brennand**, Head of Procurement, Peel Airports Limited

To read any of these testimonials in full, go to:

http://optimaltrack.com/testimonials_listing.php.

The Effective Leadership Guide

31 Proven Lessons to Increase Personal Effectiveness and Leave your Competition Standing

Michael Nicholas

Filament Publishing

All Rights Reserved
Copyright Michael Nicholas © MMIX

Published by
Filament Publishing Ltd
14, Croydon Road, Waddon,
Croydon, Surrey. CR0 4PA
Telephone +44 (0)20 8688 2598
Fax +44 (0)20 7183 7186
info@filamentpublishing.com

www.filamentpublishing.com

Printed and bound in Great Britain by
CPI Antony Rowe, Chippenham and Eastbourne

ISBN: 978-1-905493-27-2

All rights reserved. No portion of this book may be reproduced or transmitted in any form or by any means, mechanical or electronic, including photocopying and recording, or by any information storage or retrieval system, in whole or in part, without written consent of the author or publisher.

Companies, Organisations, Institutions, and Industry Publications:

Quantity discounts are available on bulk purchases of this book for reselling, educational purposes, subscription incentives, gifts, sponsorship, or fundraising. Special books or book excerpts can also be created to fit specific needs such as private labelling with your logo on the cover and a message from a VIP printed inside. For more information, please contact Optimal Track Ltd at contactus@optimaltrack.com.

Contents

Introduction 1

Lesson 1: Great Change Requires Great Leadership 5

Lesson 2: The Future Belongs to the Learners 8

Lesson 3: Anyone can Learn to Lead 11

Lesson 4: Emotions and Business DO Mix 14

Lesson 5: Leadership Starts at Home 18

Lesson 6: The Huge Value of Understanding Others 21

Lesson 7: Perception Creates Our World 24

Lesson 8: Helplessness Creeps in Unnoticed 27

Lesson 9: Improved Results Start in the Mind 31

Lesson 10: Environment is Not the Cause 34

Lesson 11: Don't Expect Change to be Easy 38

Lesson 12: The Game Alone is not Enough 41

Lesson 13: The Major Determinant of Success 45

Lesson 14: Expect the Best 49

Lesson 15: The Importance of Concern for Others 52

Lesson 16: The Value of Appreciation 56

Lesson 17: Know Your Destination 60

Lesson 18: Learn to Value Failure 64

Lesson 19: The Basis of Influence 68
Lesson 20: The Need for a Strong Character 71
Lesson 21: Integrity has a Central Role 74
Lesson 22: Learn to Handle Rejection 78
Lesson 23: Lead with Humility...................................... 82
Lesson 24: It's a People Business First 86
Lesson 25: The Value of a Flexible Style 89
Lesson 26: Welcome Feedback 92
Lesson 27: Organisations Must Learn Too 96
Lesson 28: Total Accountability.................................... 99
Lesson 29: Develop Strengths 103
Lesson 30: Collaboration Really Works 106
Lesson 31: Leadership is Not a Position 110
Staying on the Journey... 114
Also by Michael Nicholas:
    Being The Effective Leader............................ 115
About Michael Nicholas.. 117

Introduction

Personal and professional growth is essential for everyone. We live in turbulent times and what we learnt yesterday becomes obsolescent at an ever increasing rate.

Historically, leaders may have been able to get adequate results without ever doing anything specifically aimed at improving their leadership skills. Many were able to rely on the power of their position allied to motivational techniques based on the old philosophy of "carrot and stick." Today, all that has changed: the bar has been lifted and is continuing to rise.

The result is a widely acknowledged shortage of effective business leaders. Many people aren't getting great results yet continue to do the same things over and over, without the understanding to do differently, hoping someday things will be different. But doing more of the same with even greater intensity isn't the answer. Being willing to change is the only way to create improved results.

My intention in writing this book is to offer some essential principles of leadership to enable you to thrive, even in times of uncertainty. I'll provide you with a style of leadership that will help you to deal effectively with the current generation of workers – the knowledge workers who know more about their particular job than their bosses do – empowering you and your team to achieve far more.

The prerequisite is that you are prepared to learn. There is an old axiom, "To earn more you must learn more." This is demonstrably true. The most highly regarded and rewarded in almost every field are those who have developed their expertise to the highest levels through study and practice-enhanced experience.

Let's not get side-tracked by focusing exclusively on earning though. Life is more than just a pay cheque and there are lots of great reasons to learn. Earning is simply one of the most obvious and measurable.

The most important benefit that I hope you will gain as a result of reading this book is a greater sense of fulfilment and happiness – the greatest prize of all.

Be prepared to take on some new activities and to approach old ones in new ways. That is the basis of learning. Every area where you, consciously or subconsciously, assume that you already know the best approach potentially limits your personal growth.

To really learn you will need to do things differently and be open to new suggestions and ideas. This means getting out of your comfort zone and changing behaviour.

People often ask, "Can executives really change their behaviour?" The answer is obviously yes. Contrary to what many people believe, we all continue to change throughout our lives. The only difference lies in the speed at which we do so and whether the change is approached proactively or only when undesirable external events demand it of us.

Personal change represents a huge opportunity. Even a small positive change in behaviour from someone at or near the top of an organisation can have a big impact, in two ways:

- Direct benefits arising from improved skills.

- Less tangible benefits created as others see an executive trying to change.

From the business perspective the second of these areas may be more important because of the encouragement it provides to others to do the same.

The key message here is, "To help others develop – start with yourself." Effective business leadership is underpinned by well developed self-leadership.

This book is full of advice on attitudes and behaviours that will help you to become more effective in running your business or team. It summarises many of the most powerful principles that have consistently been of benefit to my clients in improving their results.

There is no single best way to get the maximum benefit from the book. However, there is a worst way – and that is to read it from cover to cover in a couple of sessions and then to put it onto the book shelf!

As you may already recognise, new behaviours need to be underpinned by changes to the way that the subconscious mind operates. One of the simplest and most powerful ways that you can make that happen is through repetition.

The book contains 31 lessons, each covering a key element of leadership. I recommend that you fully familiarise yourself with only one lesson per day to gain maximum benefit from the new ideas you are absorbing. If it suits you better, take longer. The most critical element is that you take some time to reflect on each of the success principles presented in the lessons and consciously seek ways to incorporate them into your behaviours.

One of the biggest and the most common barriers to development is procrastination. Even when people know how to do better, few actually make a sustained attempt to put what they know into practice. Yet it is also perfectly obvious that if we do not start, we cannot possibly succeed in personal development.

How much you get out of this book is entirely up to you. Enjoy reading it and, more importantly, resolve to follow its principles. They will not only greatly enhance your leadership skills – you will have a lot more fun into the bargain.

Lesson 1: Great Change Requires Great Leadership

The business environment is much tougher now than it was even a short time ago and the pace of change is accelerating every year. If we aren't changing at least as quickly we will certainly be left behind.

To keep pace, businesses need strong leaders. Leadership – one description of which is the act of providing vision and influencing others to follow it – is the surest means of improving business results.

Why are leaders under greater pressure now than previously?

Leadership and change are inseparable. Therefore, economic, social, and political changes constantly place new demands on leaders. For example:

- Many people think we are now entering a new era in economic development, with *The Age of the Mind*, also called *The Age of Thinking*, replacing the Information Age. This is having a radical effect on the skill sets required by businesses and on the expectations of employees.

- Computers, the Internet and technological advances in general, continue to have a dramatic influence, changing the way that business is conducted.

- Organisations are becoming increasingly decentralised. More and more people are working from home and the global market place is operating around the clock.

Let's start by recognising that such changes are completely natural. The universe is in constant motion: from the changing of the seasons to the ebb and flow of the oceans; from the birth and death of whole industries to shifting preferences of different generations. Life is always moving, always changing. In fact, the only constant in the world, the only thing you can absolutely count on, is change itself.

As a result, the ability to find opportunity in change has always been one of the prerequisites of true leadership. It requires leaders to stay attuned to the developments taking place around them and respond in an effective manner.

Furthermore, faster change requires greater leadership skill. Anyone who is ineffective in implementing change will not stay ahead for long in the current market.

How can you best facilitate change?

In the modern world, to get stronger on a sustainable basis a company has to maximise the effectiveness of its employees. To do this, company leaders will need to stimulate thought and encourage the development of different competencies.

Unlike professionals in almost every other field, for whom extensive training and practice is the route to success, most leaders have put relatively little conscious effort into developing their own skills. Also, their early grounding was most likely in developing technical/functional skills and knowledge. By the time they needed to learn to lead others, the daily work pressures were often too great for skill development to be seen as a priority.

The good news is that leadership can be learnt. All of the necessary competencies can be developed with practice. This offers a huge opportunity to get ahead for anyone who is prepared to focus additional effort into learning the necessary skills.

What skills provide the strongest foundation?

As economic change gathers pace, or as individual careers progress, personal and interpersonal skills become increasingly critical. The higher you want to climb, the greater your need to develop outstanding interpersonal skills.

Ultimately, your impact will be determined by your ability to influence and inspire others. Unless you know how to lead – yourself and others – you are likely to become a barrier to, rather than a catalyst for, change.

Success Principle

"Only those capable of implementing change effectively will stay ahead. This requires very strong leadership."

Lesson 2: The Future Belongs to the Learners

The previous lesson introduced the idea that the ability to learn well is essential – and becoming ever more so to allow us to respond to the accelerating pace of change that we are all now facing.

Unfortunately, few people really understand the requirements of effective learning. We typically develop our skills to an adequate level, then move on to the next essential, pressing, or urgent task. The skills we were previously working on then receive no conscious development until external events dictate that a higher level of expertise is essential. They become habitual and unconscious – even if they are ineffective or inadequate to get us to our goals.

Despite the fact that this pattern frequently results in the acceptance of mediocre standards, it is rare for people to pursue learning with energy and commitment.

Why is learning so essential for leaders in particular?

Change creates problems, which bring with them uncertainty. And, as we will go on to explore in more detail in Lesson 11, most people passionately avoid uncertainty. A feature of the ego is that it will always prefer safety and security over the untested and unproven. It likes to keep things the same.

This behaviour goes directly against the natural state of the universe. Seeking to avoid problems is a strategy that only ends in failure – they happen automatically, so the only people without them are those who are already dead!

What people who practice problem avoidance don't recognise is that the real issue is not the problem, but themselves. It is not the size of the problem that matters but your ability to handle it.

Great leaders have developed an enormous ability to handle problems, while poor leaders don't deal with them very well. There are no exceptions. The bigger the problems you can handle, the bigger the business you will have the ability to lead and the more successful you will become.

So if you want to improve your leadership, it's the size of you that matters, not the size of your problems. You must be bigger than they are and that requires ongoing learning.

What blocks growth?

Everyone has blind spots in their understanding of themselves and the world around them: it's a feature of the way the mind works. These blind spots lead to the repetition of behaviours and choices that hinder us and, most critically, by their nature most people are resistant to acknowledging them.

To grow and improve our results we must first identify our blind spots – and then address them.

The most effective way of getting the awareness that we are missing is from other people. We need to develop a willingness to receive feedback, learn and change. Even if major blind spots do not exist, we nevertheless all have opportunities for growth that reside outside our conscious awareness.

By becoming more receptive to feedback, gaining awareness and seeking growth opportunities we can accelerate the rate at which we learn.

Why is motivation important?

The motivation to learn a new behaviour comes from a desire to achieve something greater than we are doing at present. Any time we are insufficiently connected emotionally to potential long-term gain we are likely to choose instead our habitual behaviours or easier options. We will choose the immediate payoff. This happens even if, as is usually the case, the benefit of the easy option is a diminishing one.

To learn and change we must seek to achieve something that we feel sufficiently passionately about that it motivates a change in our current behaviour.

Success Principle

"Some problems will never go away so we must learn to overcome them. The magnitude of our success will be determined by the size of problems that we have learnt to handle."

Lesson 3: Anyone Can Learn to Lead

Many people feel that they don't have the potential to become a leader. There is a very well established misconception that great leaders are born with the natural aptitude necessary and that it is this that carries them to the top.

This belief is fallacious. It arises from years of conditioning that almost everyone received from other people who already held the belief. The problem becomes compounded during our early years, when most of us have a compelling need to fit in; to feel that we belong within our group.

As a result, most of us learn to become excellent followers, even if where we are heading is not to our benefit. We become like lemmings following each other blindly off a cliff to our death.

Breaking away from this conditioning is not easy. It requires that we allow ourselves to be different, to risk failure, to take a stand for something, to go first. It requires that we make the decision to become a leader.

Can anyone really learn to be a leader?

Individual perception of personal capability poses the greatest limit to expressing leadership potential. Some people may have greater natural aptitude but every competence required can be learnt! An important factor in unlocking our capability is to recognise that the most effective means of doing so is to focus on strengths.

There is no single model of leadership – many different ones have been described. So how do we choose which to follow?

Simply recognise that the enormous range of effective leadership styles – from Gandhi, to Churchill, to Jack Welch, to Richard Branson, and many more – is the result of these people developing their style according to their own strengths. We should therefore create our own individual brand of leadership.

It is always tempting to look at the finished article and believe they must always have had the skills that we admire. But this is not the case. By studying the lives of great leaders it is easy to see the mistakes they made along the way and how they learnt from them. In doing so they grew to become the people that we now recognise.

What is the first step?

The first step to being an effective leader is to realise that leadership is not restricted to the few people at the top. Anyone can decide to become one of those people who have a real influence on everything they are involved in. This is true whether they are the positional leader or not!

The single most important factor is being prepared to make the decision to be the best that we can be – to be prepared to lead rather than follow. Having made this decision, by developing our own personal talents it is possible for us to reach a high level of leadership skill no matter where we are right now.

Once anyone realises that they can make a difference, once they say, "I can", they are ready to go.

How do you overcome inertia?

Poor leadership perpetuates itself, in the workplace and elsewhere, because so many people have neither had formal training nor had good role models. It is an uncomfortable fact that many leaders simply fly by the seat of their pants. Their first experience of leading is when they are appointed to a leadership position. By simply copying others they then will tend to lead as they have been led in the past.

Breaking this pattern requires putting into practice what people in other fields of expertise do automatically. That is to seek to learn from experts while at the same time developing their own particular talents. Having started this way they maintain this approach for as long as they want to remain at the top.

Success Principle

"Leadership is a skill that can be learnt, but maximising potential is dependent upon developing natural strengths."

Lesson 4: Emotions and Business DO Mix

For many people, the idea that business leaders should become interested in emotions, VERY interested in fact, is counter-intuitive. Haven't we been taught that emotions are a sign of weakness, something that we should avoid and suppress? And, we have probably been led to believe, they certainly have little place in business.

The problem is that while we might consciously hold those thoughts, the emotions, which are generated in the subconscious, continue to happen anyway.

Most sportsmen and women would readily acknowledge that the ability to manage emotions is critical to success. The fact is that this is just as important in business. Managing mood is crucial to performance, and the tougher the trading conditions the more important it becomes.

Leaders are presented with an even greater challenge, because it is not only their own mood they must be able to manage, but also that of the people they are seeking to influence. For this, they must become very intelligent about emotions.

What is Emotional Intelligence?

Emotional Intelligence (EI) is the ability to be intelligent about emotions in ourselves and others. Its principle is that emotions convey information which can be understood and it has the following main elements:

- Self-awareness: observing yourself and becoming aware of your feelings as they are happening.

- Managing emotions: handling feelings so that behaviours remain appropriate and supportive of desired outcomes.

- Motivating oneself: channelling emotions towards a goal, having emotional self-control, delaying gratification, and stifling impulses.

- Recognising emotions in others: sensitivity to others' feelings and concerns and appreciating the differences in how people feel about things.

- Handling relationships: influencing emotions in others, social competence and social skills.

Business problems are more often a test of character than of business acumen. It is emotional skills that allow leaders to overcome the challenges that they face without derailing their projects.

Why are emotions so critical?

Every day we make very many decisions. Fortunately we have the ability to do this almost entirely subconsciously, based on a lifetime of learning that our enormously powerful subconscious mind can draw on at any time. With a little reflection we can easily recognise most of these decisions as habits.

The vital role of emotions is that they are actually the way that we experience what is going on in our subconscious. They give us conscious awareness of whether we are in an empowering or a disempowering frame of mind. If we are experiencing any negative emotion, and things like anger, frustration and resentment definitely fall into this category, it will have an adverse effect on every decision we make.

Most people would be familiar with how easily just one negative thought can undermine the performance of a sportsman. This is why it is so critical for world-class athletes to master emotional control.

The same is equally true in business. Essentially, human beings are emotional creatures – meaning that our decisions are driven by our emotions. No one can perform at their best unless they are feeling good.

Therefore, emotions are not something for leaders to avoid. Instead there are huge benefits to be gained from embracing them: they will help you gain the most from any situation that arises.

Which is greater, EI or IQ?

Before we get too carried away emphasising the importance of emotional intelligence, let's make sure that we keep it fully in context. Emotional intelligence is not a substitute for cognitive ability and vice versa. You need to be analytical and practical in your cognitive efforts, too. These are actually synergistic, with top performers having both.

The key point is that leaders need to be able to make a contribution through other people. This requires emotional intelligence, which is barely taught even on leadership courses.

To become successful in this area you have to be able to recognise your own feelings and those of others, and to use this awareness to manage both your emotions and your relationship with others.

Success Principle
"Having a great understanding of the powerful role of emotions in the workplace, and being able to use this to their advantage, is one of the hallmarks of great leaders."

Lesson 5: Leadership Starts at Home

The mood of a leader has a huge impact on the performance of the people he or she deals with.

Positive, upbeat and supportive behaviours stemming from good moods can powerfully energise others to give their best. On the other hand, the unpredictability of, or anxiety and fear that can be created by, a leader who is unable to manage his or her emotions effectively will undermine both performance and productivity.

If you want to become more effective at leading others, the starting point is to develop your ability to lead yourself. It is this that will allow you to stop the way that you feel from being controlled by external events. Once you can do that you will be able to start to respond to them in new ways, rather than being controlled by your habitual reactions.

Perhaps most important of all is the question, "If you cannot lead yourself, why should anyone else follow you?"

Why is self-awareness important?

Let's start off by considering awareness in general because it is at the foundation of all of our results. This stands to reason since results are created through actions, and no one can take action without some level of awareness of what needs to be done. Anyone lacking awareness of how to approach a certain situation is powerless to deal with it.

To use a metaphor, it may be very hard to navigate at street level in a strange city, even if your chosen destination is a major landmark. However, if you were to climb a tall building, even though nothing had changed at street level, your current location and destination would become clear and you would immediately know which way to head. You would have a different level of awareness of your situation provided by the different viewpoint.

Thus, as your awareness grows, the way that you see things will change enabling you to recognise more effective courses of action.

The most important aspect of awareness is self-awareness. As long as 2,500 years ago Socrates advised, "Know thyself." Yet rarely is the value of this piece of advice fully appreciated.

Self-awareness is critical because it is the foundation upon which self-leadership and all other people-related leadership skills depend. It is about recognising your strengths and weaknesses, being prepared to look proactively for your own flaws and opportunities for growth, and then taking responsibility for handling them accordingly. It enables you to understand the reasons why you take the actions that you do and why you experience the emotions that you feel.

As we have already covered in Lesson 2, anything that you are unaware of, your blind spots, will control you and will, until recognised, be impossible to change. Self-awareness is therefore a prerequisite for self-leadership and is the foundation on which all other leadership skills depend.

How does self-awareness support self-leadership?

A study by two of the founders of emotional intelligence, Peter Salovey and John Mayer, found that people with a greater ability to identify and give a name to their moods also had the ability to recover more quickly when upset.

Once you are able to recognise your emotions and let the negative ones go, it frees you from being controlled by them. By becoming more self-aware, you open up the possibility of shifting your state from a negative emotion to a positive alternative, such as enthusiasm. This makes a huge difference to how well you will deal with people and challenges.

The real goal here is to be able to maintain a responsive rather than reactive state. This means being able to break away from habitual behaviours based on external circumstances to create the ability to make new choices. It is not possible to get new results from old habits.

Habitual behaviours become most prevalent when people are in a poor emotional state. Ironically, the reason for the poor state is most likely self-doubt about their ability to deal with the situation they face – so what is absolutely essential at such times is a new response. Yet this is precisely what the state itself prevents from happening: a classic vicious circle.

In contrast, the responsiveness enabled by strong self-leadership will allow you to assess the situation calmly and to identify the most appropriate course of action.

Success Principle

"Improving self-leadership is critical if you want to improve your results. It is not possible to lead others effectively unless you are first prepared to lead yourself."

Lesson 6: The Huge Value of Understanding Others

In the previous lesson I mentioned that self-awareness, as well as being key to self-leadership, is also the foundation for all people-orientated leadership skills. This is because it also enables a much closer connection to the motivations of others.

If you explore deeply enough, everyone is motivated to achieve the same things: one model for this with which you may be familiar is Maslow's Hierarchy of Needs. This means that as you come to understand yourself better you will automatically gain understanding of others, and vice versa.

Through gaining better understanding of others it becomes possible to find ways to influence them which tap into their deepest motivators. For example, in survey after survey it has been found that, at work, the desire for good relationships with colleagues, the ability to learn, and the ability to contribute are consistently the top three motivators.

Pay and money are well down the list.

By understanding more about the reasons why people behave as they do we can also become more compassionate about their challenges. We will then naturally deal with them in a more empowering way.

What is the role of empathy?

An important element in understanding others is empathy, the ability to understand how someone else is likely to be feeling in any particular situation. It is crucial for leadership.

Researchers have known for years that empathy definitely contributes to occupational success. People who are best at identifying the emotions of others are more successful in their work as well as in their social lives.

Empathy helps you put yourselves into another person's place and understand what they are feeling. It enables you to put aside your own views and values for a time, and to consider a situation from another perspective.

How can understanding help leaders manage conflict?

Understanding people from an empathetic perspective will dramatically improve your ability to deal with them effectively allowing you to find much more comprehensive solutions. Most cases of resentments and misunderstandings are the result of communication issues which could have been avoided or resolved by fully understanding the other person's point of view.

The first hurdle we must overcome when conflict arises is to avoid becoming emotionally involved ourselves. We must not allow it to trigger automatic negative responses of our own.

If we react with intolerance and negativity to anything that is happening around us we instantly lose our ability to empathise. Our ability to interact effectively with the people involved is then immediately compromised.

By improving our understanding of why others behave in the way that they do we gain the ability to manage our reaction to them.

So cognitive function can shape our own emotions?

To a degree.

In fact, the functions of thinking and feeling are handled by different parts of the brain. I mentioned earlier in the book that it is the emotional part that controls us, and it is important to realise that no amount of logic or reasoning can override these feelings. This is true irrespective of how intellectual you may be.

That said, reasoning can act as a buffer to our raw emotions and, over time, thinking differently about others will lead to a change in our behaviours towards them.

While we can never fully understand what may be going on in the mind of another person, developing a higher level of understanding of what drives their behaviours will build on your own foundation of self-awareness in an extremely powerful way. The combination of these two areas has a synergetic impact on your self-leadership capability.

Success Principle

"Understanding why people behave as they do improves both self-leadership and ability to influence others. This strengthens relationships and improves overall leadership capability."

Lesson 7: Perception Creates our World

How we feel is dependent purely upon an interpretation of reality. No event, no circumstance, no object is anything until we put a label on it. Let me provide some evidence for these statements because it will make a real difference to you if you accept this.

First, some questions: Do you find a roller coaster exhilarating or terrifying? Is a desire for wealth greedy, a great way to stimulate personal growth, or an enabler to a life of philanthropy? Do relationships bring love and happiness or misery and loss of independence? Are children the greatest blessing or a source of problems?

Whatever your position on any of these questions, it is important to realise that others will have a different perspective. No one is "correct". The differences of opinion arise purely from the way that different people interpret what is happening and, in particular, what it means to them.

So is it not possible to be certain what is right and what is wrong?

Right and wrong are interpretations based on looking at an event or situation in a particular context. Change the context and the interpretation will change.

For example, to take an extreme case, let's look at the question: is it wrong for one human being to kill another?

This is not possible to answer without considering the context in which the killing was to place. Most would say that to shoot someone in the street would be wrong. Now, what about if that person was in your home at night, uninvited? In some countries that would be completely acceptable. In others, not. And how about if that person had a knife to the throat of a loved one? Most people would consider shooting them in those circumstances to be a reasonable use of force.

This is not to say that anything goes – society needs rules around what is acceptable behaviour. Rather, it is recognition of the importance of context. It is thought provoking to note that what is considered acceptable now may well not be considered so as society moves forward and the context changes.

We make our interpretations of right and wrong based on our own internal belief systems, many of which will be completely unconscious. Yet, though they are subconscious, they powerfully influence our behaviour. They determine how well we function in each situation we face.

How, then, should beliefs be evaluated?

The important question is not really whether a belief is right or wrong, but whether it serves us and the people around us. Does the way that you interpret things lead you to take empowering actions that support you and others in the pursuit of your goals, or does it lead to sabotaging behaviours?

The critical thing to recognise in mulling over that question is that not all interpretations are equal. To be successful we must manage our emotional state in order to be able to respond, rather than react, to the situations that we face. As we have already covered, this frees us to take new, creative actions as opposed to being constrained by our habits.

Once we understand this, it is simple enough to use our conscious, reasoning capability to begin to change our beliefs and to deliberately choose those that serve us.

How is this relevant to leadership?

Anything that we judge to be wrong is very likely to have a negative impact on our ability to shape the world we live in because it will automatically create stress for us.

Instead, by choosing to see situations as opportunities rather than threats we put ourselves in a position of control over the thing that matters most – our own mood. By seeing things in a positive way we reduce the ability of external events to control the way that we feel. Lesson 5 on self-leadership described why this is so important to leaders.

We have the ability to change the way that we feel simply by reinterpreting the situation we are experiencing. By doing so, anyone has the potential to perform at a higher level. In this way we can remove any power that things outside ourselves have to control how we think, feel and act. In the process we become true leaders.

We will examine the power of beliefs further in the next lesson.

Success Principle

"Our perception literally creates the world as we experience it and thereby determines the way that we behave in it. By changing our interpretations our results will change automatically."

Lesson 8: Helplessness Creeps in Unnoticed

To be an effective leader, one of the keys is to understand that every choice we make is influenced by very deep conditioning in our minds. In other words, what stops people from doing things that they know would help them to be more effective is the subconscious beliefs that they have about themselves.

One of the most easily observed examples of the impact of this conditioning arises when people have been on training courses. Rarely do they implement what they have learnt on an ongoing basis – in fact, studies indicate that long-term benefits are gained less than 10% of the time.

To know how to change our conditioning it is first necessary to understand what it is and how it got there in the first place.

What is conditioning?

Since the day that we were born we have been picking up beliefs about the world. Initially, almost all of them were learnt from someone else. As we progress through life we increasingly become shaped by our experiences. All of these lessons are stored in the subconscious mind, integrated with our natural preferences, and acted on automatically from then on.

This conditioning is so pervasive and powerful that it shapes every decision we make. Furthermore, because it is largely subconscious it is impossible to fully recognise how profoundly it impacts us.

Take the following example of how deeply our choices are influenced even by smells. Pheromones are chemicals produced by the body which produce a specific reaction in others. Men produce a pheromone called Exaltolide, which is attractive to women. In a study, trace amounts of it were placed on chairs in college classrooms and waiting rooms. It was found that men avoided these chairs, whilst women displayed a preference for them. Despite the fact that the smell was imperceptible consciously it nevertheless shaped behaviours and choices in a significant way.

How does conditioning create helplessness?

Examples of how conditioning creates helplessness are easy to observe in other creatures:

- The elephant that can be restrained by a 12-inch stake in the ground, even though it clearly has many times the physical strength needed to pull out the stake. It learnt as a youngster that the chain attaching it to a strong tree could not be broken. Having adopted this belief, the most flimsy of restrains will keep him captive for the rest of his life.

- The pike that will swim at the opposite end of a tank to a number of smaller fish. At one time a glass divide separated them, and once the pike has learnt that it cannot reach its prey it no longer tries to do so even after the glass has been removed.

- Fleas contained in an open-top tank that they could easily jump out of. Initially the tank had a lid. Once the fleas had learnt to jump low enough to avoid hitting the lid, the lid was no longer required.

In all of these cases the actual limitation on behaviour resides entirely in the mind.

Exactly the same process of conditioning has been proven to take place in humans. To some degree we have all learnt to jump lower than we are capable of doing. Our biggest limitation is simply that we don't realise it.

How can learned helplessness be overcome?

Most of the time we are not actively choosing how to behave. Our actions are unconscious, dictating that we live almost all of our lives habitually and on autopilot.

Beliefs are so powerful in controlling behaviour that if you believe you can do something, you will probably turn out to be right. Unfortunately, the opposite is also true. In effect, the main thing that prevents us from getting the things we want is the reasons we give ourselves why we can't have them.

This is great news. It means that we have within us the capability to improve all of our results in life by understanding, and changing, the beliefs that we have about ourselves that limit us. We must remove our limiting beliefs and replace them with new ones that serve us.

As a leader it is especially important that you do this. One of the most powerful ways to do so is to examine the way you evaluate things, as described in the previous lesson. You must also help those you work with through the process. Many of the lessons later in this book can assist you with this.

Success Principle

"The biggest thing preventing people from achieving all that they are capable of is their own limiting beliefs, most of which are outside their conscious awareness. These must be identified and removed."

Lesson 9: Improved Results Start in the Mind

Let me start by making a statement: everything that exists in modern society, from the material things that we have created, to our laws and social agreements, to the most beautiful classical symphony – everything – originated in the mind.

If you don't agree with this statement then I urge you to give it some consideration because it is a fundamental point. It provides the basis for all progress, for yourself, your team, or your business.

To put it another way, everything that man have ever created started as an idea in someone's mind. If you want to improve your results this is the only really effective place to start. All advancement relies for its conception on the ability to think differently.

Can the mind really be improved?

There is a widely held and highly detrimental belief that even a healthy mind becomes weaker with age, losing its creativity, memory function and learning capacity. Fortunately, it is now known that this belief is completely wrong.

The thing that causes the brain to deteriorate, unless disease is present, is actually lack of activity, not ageing. What you don't use, you lose. In fact, we now know that the brain creates new brain cells throughout our whole lives to replace those that we lose.

Just as the body can be strengthened, toned and gain in endurance capability through regular use and activity, so it is with the mind. The world's greatest memory experts did not start out that way – they developed their capability through practice (combined with systems and techniques). If you continue to keep your mental processes active by challenging yourself to solve problems and think in new ways, then it is extremely likely that your mind will serve you well for the rest of your life.

I described in detail in my first book, *Being The Effective Leader* (available from www.beingtheeffectiveleader.com), the latest scientific thinking about the true potential of our mind. This has concluded that there is no practical limitation to our ability to generate thoughts. Acceptance of this fact alone is sufficient to increase your ability to unlock your potential and that of the people you work with.

Garbage in, garbage out?

An important feature of the mind is that it is synergetic. This means that as we add more information to it the total increases by more than the amount added. While this can work in our favour, it also means that we must be very careful what we feed our mind with.

In some important ways the mind can be compared to a farmer's field. The land does not care what gets planted in it, be it crops or weeds. It will allow to grow whatever it is given. If a farmer wants a field of healthy crops he must tend them and prevent the weeds from gaining hold. Without such care the field quickly returns to nature, and the farmer would have little prospect of earning a living from it.

The mind behaves similarly, except that the mind is many times more productive than the most fertile soil. Because of its extraordinary creativity and its synergetic nature, whatever is placed in the mind will be magnified and grow. Negative thought patterns are as readily accepted as positive ones and can quickly expand to dominate our actions. If we put garbage in, it will be amplified to give us even more garbage in return.

Great attention and care should therefore be taken over what thoughts are allowed to take up space in your mind. If you want great results you must constantly seek to feed your mind with information and ideas that will help it to grow.

Success Principle

"Everything created by man originated as an idea in the mind, so it is possible to radically transform your results and those of your team by focusing on developing the mind."

Lesson 10: Environment is Not the Cause

The last few lessons have outlined the importance of the mind in shaping results and touched on the role of our thoughts in this process. Now, I want to look at thoughts in more detail.

Most people experience the world through their 5 senses, believing that this gives them a reliable representation of "what is". However, it does not, because of the way that the subconscious mind works.

What happens in practice is that we filter the information available to us such that we prove to ourselves that what we already believe is correct.

How does our subconscious filtering work?

The problem arises because of the enormously greater power of our subconscious in comparison to our conscious mind. Some have estimated it to have around a million times as much processing power.

As a result, the subconscious is able to receive and evaluate far more information from the outside world than we are capable of processing consciously. To reduce the conscious load to a level that we are capable of handling a huge amount of filtering is required. The result is that we delete huge chunks of the information that arrives in our subconscious mind, generalising and distorting it prior to conscious awareness.

This filtering is incredibly significant because of the way that prioritisation of the information to be brought to conscious awareness is done. There is a particular part of the brain which is responsible, known as the Reticular Activating System, and it filters all your subconscious data based on *your existing beliefs about what is important to you.*

What is the impact of the filtering process?

Because of the way that we process data, it is not really possible for us to know what "reality" is. As soon as we have formed a belief it is inevitable that we will prove that we are right, irrespective of the evidence to the contrary. Our internal filter simply blocks out anything that is inconsistent with the belief, reinforcing what we already hold to be true and labelling it as "real".

This makes it hard for our awareness to grow. We have expressions like, "I'll believe it when I see it," which reflect most people's natural resistance when faced with a new idea. In practice, the process of discovery works the other way around. It is impossible to see anything that is not consistent with your existing conditioning; in other words, you will only see it after you believe it.

This process can have a huge impact in business. Resistance to new ideas does not necessarily mean that people are being awkward or territorial (though this can happen). It is more likely that they cannot even recognise opportunities to change because their mind is blocking them out.

A powerful example of how this trait can even affect large groups of people occurred when the Wright Brothers completed their first flight. The general public refused to believe that it actually happened, irrespective of what they were told, for a further 5 years.

How can we benefit from awareness of the mind's filtering?

The first stage is to recognise how people's minds typically interact with the world:

1. Thinking creates the beliefs in the subconscious mind that we experience as feelings.

2. Feelings determine actions.

3. Actions produce results.

4. We observe the results through our 5 senses, becoming aware of those that are consistent with existing beliefs.

5. Further thinking is dominated by input from the senses, in other words our current results, reinforcing the beliefs that created them. We then automatically repeat the actions that took place in step 2 and become stuck.

Because most people don't understand that thoughts initiate the process, when their results don't please them they will always be able to find reasons outside themselves why they happened. By doing so they give away all of their power to improve them. As the old saying goes, you will either have reasons or results!

To change our results we must change our thinking. This requires that we develop the capability to hold thoughts that support our goals, ignoring current results as we do so.

This is one of the characteristics of successful people: their thinking is not determined by what happens to them. This enables them to choose a new response, not based on their current conditioning or results, and creates the possibility of real growth and development.

Success Principle

"If you see the external world as the cause of your results you will severely limit your ability to create effective or rapid change in your life or to realise more of your potential. As a leader you will also block others from doing so."

Lesson 11: Don't Expect Change to be Easy

Change can be hard to bring about. It may seem intimidating. New ideas can be difficult to sell to others. People procrastinate on getting started. And, no matter how well intentioned your plan, there will be those who seem dead set against it.

The fact that our environment typically shifts only gradually on a day-to-day basis can also make the need for change hard to recognise. The millions of habits that prevent our conscious mind from becoming overwhelmed can also prevent us from noticing when our activities become ineffective.

Why is change difficult?

One of the most basic human needs is the need for certainty because it links to our deep drive to survive. A simple example of this is that if you were not certain that the building you worked in was structurally sound you would refuse to set foot in it.

Unfortunately, certainty is most easily found in the comfort zone. Our tendency is to continue to do things that are not working because they are comfortable for us; meanwhile the situation that we are in may be becoming progressively worse. Something that we would not tolerate if it occurred suddenly we often accept when it develops slowly. The slow and steady increase in pain or the accumulation of unproductive habits seemingly numbs us because of our natural desire to hold on to what we know.

At the deepest level we are all motivated by just two things: the desire to move towards pleasure and the need to avoid pain.

It is hard to recognise the pleasure to be gained from change because, having never had the experience, we lack the awareness of what it will be like afterwards. For example, someone who has never been physically fit could not possibly know how good that feels, so that awareness could not help in motivating them to start an exercise regime. Pleasure tends instead to be attached to the familiar.

On the other hand, anything new is likely to immediately have pain associated with it because it threatens our certainty. Consequently, as people step outside their comfort zone they will experience fear.

Change, therefore, may have little pleasure associated with it, but lots of pain, so most people will naturally seek the certainty of what they already know.

What can break this pattern?

Without the power to break this pattern we are powerless to improve our lives or to influence change in others. There are three main ways in which an interruption can happen:

1. The situation becomes unbearable. At some point, as the pain of the situation escalates, it becomes greater than the pain associated with changing.

2. We experience some sort of disruptive event that shocks us into changing. In this case we may suddenly become aware of where our current habits will lead us, creating pain and catalysing change.

3. We raise our level of awareness of greater possibilities and deliberately choose a better way forward. This can be stimulated at any time through education and learning.

Clearly, by far the best of these three mechanisms is to raise awareness. It leads to a proactive approach to life where choices become based on seeking what we want, rather than avoiding that which we don't.

How can we raise awareness to implement change?

Because of the power of the Reticular Activating System (see Lesson 10), even recognising the need for personal change can be difficult. We will tend to block out information that is not consistent with our own self-image because to do otherwise creates pain. As a result, we all have blind spots to things that limit our progress, even if they are completely obvious to others.

Feedback from others is by far the fastest way to learn how to progress more quickly. This will require a safe environment to be created, so that the feeling of certainty is not too threatened, which is one of the reasons why having a mentor or coach can be so incredibly valuable.

Success Principle

"Almost everyone is naturally motivated to avoid change because of the pain that they associate with it. This must be tackled proactively if personal or corporate change initiatives are to be effective."

Lesson 12: The Game Alone is not Enough

It is often said that success is just a collection of habits; unfortunately so is failure. The thing that enables world-class performers to develop the skills necessary to reach the top is the discipline of their daily routine that embeds success habits firmly into their subconscious.

Athletes understand this process. It would be inconceivable for a winning team to decide, "Ok, now that we are the best we can stop our practice." However, it would be equally impossible to imagine the struggling teams making this decision either. They all understand the vital role of practice. It is here that new skills are developed and existing ones improved.

Learning a new skill is a particular challenge. Initially it requires an enormous amount of conscious effort to displace old habits. This effort must be maintained until the new practice becomes habitual – only then can peak performance be achieved.

Why is skill development a problem for leaders?

Athletes spend a lot of time practicing and very little time performing. So do musicians and many others who must be able to perform at their peak on demand. They know it is not possible for them to delay an event because they are feeling off-form.

In business the demands of the job make it practically impossible to take this approach. Leaders spend most of their time on the playing field, too embroiled in the day-to-day challenges of meeting their objectives to focus on developing themselves.

Yet it will often be just as important for business leaders to perform on demand as it is for an athlete and they must constantly improve their skills to stay ahead.

Lesson 3 introduced the idea that, very often, executives learn most of what they know about leading others after they are promoted into their first leadership role. They are likely to spend some time watching role models around them, but unless they have spent time working out what great leadership really looks like they may not even know if what they are learning will get them past average capability. And I don't know anyone who wants to be average!

Having developed their skills to an adequate level few people devote sufficient effort to ongoing growth to enable themselves to excel. This may contribute to the shortage of high-quality leadership which is consistently identified by surveys.

What is the solution?

There are many things we do daily that we accept as requirements for a healthy life, such as eating, keeping ourselves clean, and maintaining our living environment. We know that none of these activities has a lasting effect and we unquestioningly accept the need to repeat them on a frequent basis.

If you want to be able to create outstanding results as a leader it is essential to adopt this attitude to your personal development. It may require some reprioritisation of effort, but the synergetic nature of the brain will ensure that with proper application the rewards will far outweigh the effort involved.

In a nutshell, you must regularly spend time working on your leadership skills.

Is there anything that can speed up the process?

The more often that a new behaviour is exercised the more strongly the new neural circuits associated with it will develop and the more automatic it will become.

One way to speed up the process is the use of visualisation techniques. The subconscious mind cannot tell the difference between something that is actually happening and something that we vividly imagine – hence the reason that the memory of an old hurt can inflame the emotions, possibly even more so than when the original event occurred.

Visualisation was the technique used by Roger Bannister to help him believe that it was possible to break the 4-minute mile. It is still used today by athletes and performers in every field to accelerate success.

This process can be just as effective in business. Every time you visualise the attainment of a new behaviour or goal it reinforces new pathways in the subconscious, overwriting old habits and gradually installing the new ones needed to produce the desired result.

Success Principle

"Very few people make significant progress without first being prepared to put in additional effort towards personal growth. To achieve excellence you will need to make this a regular practice."

Lesson 13: The Major Determinant of Success

The previous lesson introduced the idea that for anyone to create outstanding results they must be able to produce high performance on demand. It is not enough to be able to perform well some of the time – they must do it all of the time. For example, this attribute is what distinguishes world-class professional speakers from the rest. A relatively large number of people may produce occasional presentations to their standard, but the professionals can do it every time.

We can sum up what creates this ability to perform on demand with one word: attitude. It is critical to self-leadership.

Attitude is the composite of all of our thoughts, feelings and actions. Above all other areas of capability, it determines how successful we will be in life. It particularly affects whether we see the best or the worst in a situation, interpreting it as opportunity or threat, and whether we will react out of habit or respond with awareness. It shapes all of our results and determines our destiny.

How is your leadership affected by your attitude?

The most important aspect of our attitude in leadership is how we relate to people.

Success in business is much more about people than product. The relationships built through the course of a career are essential to the success of that career – no one does it alone. Whatever industry or functional skill area you work in, an estimated 85% of the skills needed at senior levels are people skills (and even in the most technical jobs, such as research scientists, this figure is still 50%).

What do you really think of the people you are leading? Your beliefs will impact your relationships in every interaction because they determine how you treat others. As in every other area, the actions and behaviours that you choose are dependent on your subjective interpretation of the people around you: of your "reality" as it relates to them.

The question that few people stop to consider is whether their interpretation, and the subsequent behaviour that it induces, actually serves them. For example, if someone who works for you does not achieve a set task and you have a tendency to get angry, does this anger move you towards or away from your goals? Or is there another way that you could achieve your outcome in a more positive way? My experience, personally and working with my clients, is that there always is.

How can we develop a great attitude?

Emotions provide the key to developing the optimal performance state.

There are many reasons why most people pay their emotions limited attention – too many to go into here – but the important point to recognise is that our emotions are a normal response that has developed over tens of millions of years in order to help us to thrive. They don't just happen, but are accompanied by a chemical change throughout the body and have a huge impact on our behaviour.

I mentioned the importance of feedback in Lesson 2 and will cover different aspects of it in detail in Lessons 18 & 26. If we ignore our emotions we are not taking advantage of perhaps the most powerful feedback system available to us.

So, the optimal performance state is actually an emotional response. It gives us the ability to respond appropriately and adaptively to stimuli: a capability that is blocked by negative emotions. Its characteristics are things like: alert concentration, confidence, challenge, optimism, enjoyment, positive energy, calmness and a relaxed approach.

In the same way that Pavlov conditioned dogs to salivate on hearing a bell, any emotional response can be conditioned. With awareness and practice anyone can learn to produce an optimal performance state on demand.

What is at the core of the optimal performance state?

Ultimately, everyone performs best when they are happy, and happiness is critical to achieving an optimal performance state. Furthermore, happiness has also been shown to be closely linked to other areas such as job satisfaction, employee health, ability to tolerate pain and frustration, and quality of relationships.

Unfortunately, multiple studies have estimated that as few as 20% of people are genuinely happy. This represents a huge opportunity to improve business performance, and leaders can make a significant impact by engaging people in such a way that they will feel good. We will explore this area further in the next couple of lessons.

Success Principle

"To become outstanding as a leader it is essential that you develop the ability to create an optimal performance state on demand."

Lesson 14: Expect the Best

There is an enormous difference between expecting high standards which, in the context that many people use this term, is to require those that work for them to produce high quality work, and expecting the best from people.

At the root of this difference is a core belief about a leader's role: whether it is focus on getting the job done or to develop people and trust that to do so will automatically produce the best possible outcome. Anyone who does not believe in the potential of human beings is likely to adopt the former approach. (They are also likely to work long hours and find work very stressful!)

This is not to suggest for a moment that producing work to a high standard is unimportant. Quite the opposite is true. It is more a question of what you expect your team to be capable of. This matters a great deal, because your expectation has a major impact on the outcome.

Why is expectation so critical?

Numerous studies have demonstrated the link between expectation and performance. The name given to this relationship is the Pygmalion effect, or self-fulfilling prophecy. It refers to the idea that when someone creates a belief in something that is not yet true, and then expects it with certainty, it will actually happen. Once again, the natural function of the mind provides understanding of why this occurs.

It used to be believed that we react to information flowing into the mind from the outside world. This is no longer thought to be true. Instead, we have learnt that we react to what the mind, on the basis of previous experience, expects to happen next. Because we take action based on the expectation, very often we create the results that we anticipate.

In relation to people the Pygmalion effect suggests that we will communicate our expectations of others to them, following which they conform and deliver results to match expectation.

Scientific evidence that the Pygmalion effect should be taken seriously is extensive. Since Robert Rosenthal and Leonore Jacobson published the first study in this area in 1968 there have been over 700 doctoral dissertations and countless journal articles on the subject. What they have demonstrated is that what we expect is, all too often, exactly what we get.

How does the Pygmalion Effect work?

The process by which expectation gets converted into reality has three main stages:

1. We form certain expectations, or beliefs, about people and events based on our own, as yet unrealised, perceptions.

2. Those expectations get communicated through cues because we behave in a way that we would not have done without the unconscious belief.

3. Other people generally respond to these cues by adjusting their belief systems to match. Once this has happened a change in their behaviours is automatic.

The result is that the original expectations become fact.

How will the Pygmalion Effect impact me in business?

It is no coincidence that a study of 100 self-made millionaires found that one of the characteristics that they had in common was the desire and ability to see the good in others. They were people builders, not people critics.

As a leader or manager in a company, any time you express lack of confidence in others it is likely that they will return it with mediocre performance. On the other hand, if you believe in them and expect them to do well, they will usually seek to live up to that expectation. Expecting the best makes a practical difference.

Recognise that the communication through cues that takes place in stage 2 of the process is primarily subconscious. It is not so much what you say but the way in which you say it and how you behave that makes the difference. Indifferent and noncommittal treatment of staff is the kind of behaviour that communicates low expectations and leads to poor performance. So does control and micro-management.

You can help to improve the performance of staff by believing in them and creating an accepting and encouraging social and emotional environment.

Success Principle

"Leaders can stimulate higher performance from employees simply by believing in them and letting them know it."

Lesson 15: The Importance of Concern for Others

Most people blunder through life attempting to get other people to like them. There is a problem with this approach – it doesn't work. The thing that each of us is really interested in is much closer to home: our self.

Do you doubt it? Can you guess what the most common word used in telephone conversations is? You've probably anticipated the answer – it's "I." Also, contrast for a moment your mild interest in the affairs of the world with your huge interest in yourself, then realise that everyone else is the same. We even have the expression, "not in my back yard", to describe our resistance to things of benefit to the common good if they work to our own disadvantage.

I find it fascinating that the expression, "man's best friend," refers to dogs and not our human best friends. For centuries man has had a uniquely close relationship with dogs, as a working animal, for security and, perhaps most importantly, for companionship.

Dogs have no reservations about showing how pleased they are to see us. They unconditionally wag their tails and if we show them even greater attention by patting them they will bound around to show how much they appreciate it. They have no ulterior motives or hidden agendas, and the results of this approach speak for themselves.

What does this mean to you?

William James, the American psychologist and philosopher, said, "The deepest principle in human nature is the craving to be appreciated." If this is even partially true it explains why no one really listens to or cares what you know until they first feel that you care about who they are as a person.

Concern for others is at the heart of high-quality relationships. If you want to help people and have a positive impact on them the starting point is sincere appreciation of who they are. The more you can show your co-workers that you like them and have their best interests at heart, the greater will be your ability to influence them.

Does your attitude need a makeover?

We've all seen leaders with incredible charisma, whose presence is felt wherever they are. The problem is that no one blossoms in the light of someone else's huge charisma. They have to be given the opportunity to shine their own light. This is the true job of a leader, and the reason why humility is so powerfully associated with the most outstanding leaders (more in Lesson 23).

A great attitude, and one that brings fantastic results, is to love and value people, to praise effort and to reward performance. No matter how many mistakes people make, you should not let this devalue your perception of their worth as a person. If you want great relationships, always find reasons to affirm someone first and avoid confrontation.

In pursuit of money and increased shareholder value, far too many business people undervalue their employees. This attitude will rapidly communicate itself to the people affected, creating a fear-orientated environment that will never inspire anyone to give maximum commitment.

A very simple shift in attitude that I've helped my clients with many times, and which is transformational in its impact is this:

> Whenever you meet anyone else, either individually or in groups, see if you can adopt an attitude of, *"There you are"* rather than, *"Here I am."*

In other words, learn to become interest**ed** in the person you are with, rather than trying to be interest**ing** to them.

Will some people take advantage of you?

Almost certainly some will, yes. But in life that is likely to happen whatever you do. Trying to protect yourself so that nothing bad ever happens has only one guaranteed result – to leave you with a life that has not been fully lived.

A more powerful question than, "Won't some people take advantage of me?" is "Which approach will get me the best results?" For an answer to that question, take a look at the advice that has been given for thousands of years by philosophers and teachers speculating on the rules for human relationships. It is a simple ethical guideline that always provides a strong foundation for dealing with other people. Known as "The Golden Rule," it takes the form of another question:

> *"How would I like to be treated in this situation?"*

Applying this rule to the subject of this lesson, would you prefer others to show genuine interest in you or to attempt to convince you of how interesting they are?

Success Principle

"Showing a genuine interest in others is good for business. Done sincerely it creates committed employees and loyal customers."

Lesson 16: The Value of Appreciation

A powerful way to demonstrate that you care about someone else is to appreciate them. Everyone responds better when dealt with in this way.

The problem is that almost everyone has been deeply conditioned during childhood, particularly at school, to believe that appreciation had to be earned by doing well. Consequently, most people are reluctant to give appreciation in the absence of achievement.

So we may as well face it – if we want appreciation it is most likely that we will have to wait until we have done something notable. That is just how the world works – or is it?

There is an alternative approach that we can adopt towards others – and the benefits for everyone of doing so are huge. It simply involves putting into practice the idea of loving people and praising effort that was introduced in the previous lesson. This can be done through appreciation.

What if what people are doing or saying is wrong?

There a critical point to remember here: that right and wrong are interpretations based on a particular point of observation (we covered this in Lesson 7). As awareness grows, what once may have been believed with absolute certainty may now appear completely false. For example, it is now very clear that to keep Galileo under house arrest for supporting the view that the rest of the universe does not revolve around the Earth was a very unjust decision!

Other people may appear completely wrong to someone with a higher level of awareness. However, never forget that they don't think so and from their current level of awareness it is not possible for them to realise it, even if they are. Everyone is doing the best they can with the knowledge that they have available.

When they are wrong, don't they need to know it?

In many circumstances it is possible that people would benefit from a different interpretation, but the problem is that they don't know it yet. Right now they value their current opinion. Any attempt to force them to change will bring up uncertainty, which they associate with pain.

As a result, the natural reaction to challenges over what we think or do is to become defensive. They rapidly create a loss of motivation and a shift of behaviours towards being more cautious, less willing to learn and more resistant to change.

Consider the application of this idea in career development sessions, annual employee reviews, or even simply when providing feedback. The standard approach to these types of meetings is to start with something positive, then to identify the deficiencies that form the main focus of the subsequent discussion and, almost as an afterthought, to finish on a positive.

The problem with this, as so often occurs in any communications situation, is that the subconscious cues from the person "in charge" clearly indicate to the recipient what is considered to be most important – the flaws. So as soon as the conversation starts, albeit on a positive note, feelings of anxiety and defensiveness are automatically triggered.

If you are giving feedback and your focus is faults, then the recipient will feel it. This approach will not give you the ability that you need to powerfully influence others.

How can you improve your influence?

Recognise that it is easy to criticise others. It requires very little ability and is the approach often taken by insecure people who are unprepared to address their own limitations.

It may be painful initially, but I urge you to be honest with yourself about your own behaviour in this area. The way of the great leader is to seek to understand others; particularly why they hold their beliefs – your results will start to change the moment that you do more of this.

What is necessary to enable this change is a shift in your own intention in favour of a greater appreciation of others.

Start to look at the cause of behaviour, not the effect which is the behaviour itself. By becoming interested in the cause you will become progressively less likely to dislike the effect. The subconscious cues that you transmit will then become much more positive and engaging.

Finally, constantly seek to change your own perception. Apply "The Golden Rule" by asking yourself how the other person might be feeling and how you would want to be treated in those circumstances. Also, recognise your role as being to help others to raise their level of awareness. This is one of the foundational principles of coaching, and is the only way that they will be able to create better results.

Your job as a leader is to find ways to bring out more of the potential of those around you. Withholding critical comments is not enough. It is important to provide people with positive affirmation through praise or compliments.

Success Principle

"By being prepared to appreciate people as they are you will dramatically sharpen your relationship skills and transform your results."

Lesson 17: Know Your Destination

All successful leaders have a powerful vision of where they are going and a reason why they want to get there. This is essential because it is impossible to persuade anyone else to do something without first being able to describe it and being passionate about it yourself.

The "reason why" is called purpose – it is essential to ongoing achievement. A clear purpose inspires others and provides consistency of direction that unleashes the power of the conscious and subconscious towards its achievement.

Why is purpose so important?

Without a clear purpose life lacks meaning and we are likely to drift through it. There may be a great deal of activity but it will hold little interest, excitement, or fulfilment for us.

Many people have told me of having experienced the disappointment of achieving a goal and discovering that the satisfaction gained was transitory and not really worth the effort involved. What is missing here is the direction and meaning provided by the context of a higher purpose.

At a personal level, purpose impacts us in several ways. In particular, it:

- Determines how we will respond to the inevitable setbacks that we will face in life by igniting the critical element of our character called persistence. This may be the only quality that can be found in successful people which is absent in everyone else.

- Removes the confusion that many people experience when faced with tough life decisions, such as whether to accept a career move.

- Provides engagement at the emotional level by connecting us with our dreams, which is the only way that we can deliver our maximum effort.

- Provides the best motivation to learn.

The "how" of achieving a goal is not important until you know the "reason why" and that is provided by your purpose. Your "why" is your ultimate motivation. For example, Martin Luther King's purpose might have been to end racial discrimination. Purpose counteracts the fear and doubts that inevitably arise at some point as life's challenges unfold.

How can purpose be translated into daily activities?

The most important element in making your purpose tangible is to have very clear goals for its achievement. It requires the development of a very important and typically underrated mental faculty – that of imagination.

Few people maximise the value that they get from goals because of a poor understanding of how to set them effectively. There is extensive guidance on this in my book, *Being The*

Effective Leader, but for now here are two critical pieces of advice:

1. One of the most common errors in setting goals is to set them too low. Specifically, I suggest avoiding using SMART goals, with which most people are familiar, because of the error of seeking to make them "Attainable" and "Realistic". This will limit your potential.

2. Realise that a goal's main function is not the achievement of the goal itself but rather who you need to become in order to achieve it. This will always be of far greater value than what you get.

Do goals really affect performance?

There has been much research into the effectiveness of goals. Both the results of these studies and the qualitative observation that people who achieve great success almost always have clear goals support the belief that goals have a huge impact on achievement.

An important factor in why this is so stems from the way the mind works. In Lesson 10 we covered the role of the Reticular Activating System (RAS) in determining what we perceive in our environment. In summary, the RAS filters out anything that we don't already believe to be important to us to prevent overload of the conscious mind.

It is not the case that people who constantly find opportunities to bring more abundance (of all types) into their lives are lucky. They have set up their mind to seek out and recognise these opportunities by programming the RAS to look for them. A goal can make this happen.

Success Principle

"The mind is a goal-seeking organism. Whatever goal you give it, it will work to achieve even while you sleep. To benefit from this incredible power and get what you want you must be very clear in defining what you want. You must have goals."

Lesson 18: Learn to Value Failure

The achievement of goals requires you to learn. If it did not then they would be immediately achievable for you – and would not constitute worthwhile goals.

Unfortunately, most people approach learning incorrectly. They are seeking to get an improved outcome at every attempt. This is one of the reasons why so many of them don't have the persistence necessary to practice new skills for long enough to master them. They quickly fall back to their old habits and fail to benefit as they had intended when the started out.

Any time you seek to achieve a goal it will be necessary to take on something new. In other words, you will have to do things that you have not done before, so the results that you achieve will not always be as expected. There will inevitably be times when you will fail.

Not everyone seems to fail?

Not everyone is successful either.

Many people don't take action because they are too afraid of getting it wrong. They don't like the awkwardness of learning something new or the risk of failure and consequently also tend to opt out from taking on anything that would enable them to achieve a significant win.

Children don't have this problem. They are continually trying new things and are familiar and comfortable with failing.

It doesn't deter them. Most adults have lost this ability without even realising the price that they have had to pay. Ideas such as that they are, "Better safe than sorry" or that, "If I stay with what I know I won't get hurt" are so deeply embedded that they are too afraid of being wrong to ever really stretch themselves.

The problem is that staying safe is an impossible goal for anyone who wants to progress. If you want to learn something new or to get better at anything – you will have to risk failure. Those with the highest willingness to do so give themselves the greatest chance of achieving something meaningful with their life.

What is the process for effective learning?

Progress from where you are now to where you want to go will not take place in a straight line. Human learning is a trial and error process that looks like this:

1. Decide what you want – this is the goal setting process.

2. Take action to move toward your goal.

3. Notice the results of your efforts.

4. Evaluate your results against the desired outcomes and refine your actions.

5. Repeat steps 2-4 until success has been achieved.

You might have heard people say that you should not "try" anything; that you should commit and "do it" instead. In my opinion this demonstrates a lack of understanding of this process.

Trying is essential to achieving goals because it is the only way to explore new possibilities to find one that works. The most important aspect is to seek to learn with every attempt and to remain persistent until you have been successful.

Is there a more constructive way to view failure?

In Lesson 7, we explored the idea that nothing is anything until we interpret and label it based on our own experience. This provides the means of changing your whole perspective on failure.

Steps 3 & 4 above involve noticing the results of your efforts and evaluating them against your desired outcome. A single word that could be used to describe this process is "feedback". Alternatively, if the results fall short of the desired outcome, another would be "failure." These are merely labels that we apply to the situation. Which feels better to you?

Here's how I often work this through in seminars or with my clients:

> Me: "Which day feels better, the one where everything goes well or when everything seems to fail horribly?"
>
> Client: "When everything goes well."
>
> Me: "And on which of those days do you learn more?"

Client (sometimes after some thought): "When everything goes horribly."

Me: "So, on which day do you move more quickly towards your goals?"

Client: "Provided I learn from my mistakes, the day it all goes horribly."

Isn't that interesting? We have a natural tendency to attempt to create days when nothing goes wrong, yet on such occasions our learning will at best be minimal.

Provided you seek to learn, an alternative perspective on "failure" is that it could be celebrated. It provides the feedback that is essential to rapid growth and therefore accelerates your progress towards your goals.

Success Principle

"Start to think of learning as a process, not an outcome. Your attitude should be to seek to learn from every attempt, never considering the steps along the way as failure."

Lesson 19: The Basis of Influence

Lesson 17 – "Know Your Destination" – opened by saying that all successful leaders have a powerful vision of where they are going. That is the first of two prerequisites for success. The second is that they must be able to influence others to follow.

Influence is so critical to leadership that many people believe that the two are virtually synonymous. It is practically impossible to lead successfully without well-developed influencing skills.

What is influence?

Influence can be defined as, "A power affecting a person, thing, or course of events, especially one that operates without any direct or apparent effort." I feel that the most important aspect of this definition is that last part, because it is so rarely recognised.

The working environment is full of people attempting to get others to do what they want in a way that involves huge effort targeted directly at the people they are attempting to lead. This is a clear indication that their influencing skills are insufficiently developed.

Part of the challenge in seeking to influence others is the extraordinary complexity of the process by which people make choices. Lesson 8 identified the fact that there are many factors at play in every decision and that most of the time they will be below the level of conscious awareness. This explains why, so often, it is difficult for us to give a rational explanation why we continue with behaviours even when we know that they aren't serving us.

The key to powerful influence is to be able to engage the hearts and minds sufficiently that these automatic, subconscious behaviours can be overcome. As Gandhi demonstrated, monumental tasks can be achieved with little direct effort if other people can be persuaded to participate.

Can anyone learn to influence?

Influence has been studied scientifically for over half a century and a large body of research is available to help anyone to develop their skills.

Given how important persuasion is to success in leadership, it therefore seems strange that it is rare for people to focus on this aspect of their development. We've already seen that in the areas of technical and functional capability it is common to find people who have devoted many years to learning how to be effective. Perhaps we believe that we have an intuitive understanding of psychological principles gathered during our life experience and don't consider study to be necessary in this area.

This assumption is not supported by research in the field, but a consequence of it is a tendency to over rely on introspective approaches. This causes us to ask the question, "What would motivate me in these circumstances?" In doing so we limit our ability to influence to other people like us.

As a result, the ability of the average person to influence is relatively low. This immediately places them on a steep learning curve once they begin to study, so rapid improvement is possible with some focused effort. Because of its importance in leadership, the rewards to be gained from doing so are great.

Where can you start?

There are many specific techniques to improve influencing skills, some of which have already been touched on in this book. At the foundation, however, lie your own actions and words.

Influence has everything to do with who we are, not who we say we are – or even who we think we are. We can teach what we know, but it is what we are that we reproduce; therefore, whatever behaviours you display will most likely be modelled by the people you seek to influence. As such, your starting point is the set of internal beliefs, values, and rules that shape your character and thus your interaction with the world.

Success Principle

"Influence is a critical yet highly under-developed skill for most leaders. Only by first modelling the behaviours that you seek in others are you likely to inspire change in them."

Lesson 20: The Need for a Strong Character

A review of many of the writings on leadership will quickly establish that agreement on what it means is relatively rare. One point on which most of the researchers, analysts, and commentators do agree is that not only is character essential to leadership – it is at its very core.

The vital importance of character was summarised by General Norman Schwarzkopf, commander of the Coalition Forces in the Gulf War of 1991, when he said, "Leadership is a potent combination of strategy and character but if you must be without one, be without strategy."

Why is character so important?

When a leader has significant weaknesses, such as a tendency to step in and control or criticise, such flaws will usually be amplified as that individual becomes more senior in position or influence. Therefore it is essential to remove such weaknesses by developing the internal strength necessary to improve your self-leadership and hold yourself to a higher standard.

This internal strength may be called character. It is most strongly called for when things are not going well or some unexpected setback is encountered. Such circumstances also provide the best guide of the level to which a person has developed their character.

The challenge for leaders is that it is easy to be good-natured when times are easy but becomes progressively harder as the pressure climbs. This is why it can be said that character is not so much created by circumstances as it is revealed by them.

When the going gets tough is when leadership is most needed, yet this is precisely when lapses are most likely to occur as emotional self-leadership is put to the test. Few people are strong enough in other areas to allow them to be forgiven if this occurs.

What are the essential traits of character in a leader?

There are several different ways of defining character. All of them have their foundations in qualities of moral or ethical strength.

I find it most useful to consider the traits that would typically be demonstrated by great leaders. Some examples of high character behaviours or attributes are:

- Impeccability with your word, never falling short of doing what you say you will do.

- Modelling what you expect of others.

- Preparedness to be honest and open about your flaws.

- Basing your decisions on the needs of the organisation, not on your personal agenda.

- Approachability and willingness to receive feedback with an open mind.

- Treating everyone in the same way and exemplifying humility.

- Demonstrating support for others and working collaboratively.

- Demonstrating persistence in the face of difficulties.

- Preparedness to make the tough choices, especially where personal reputation or popularity could be at stake.

- The ability to manage your own emotional state as the environment around you changes.

Is character enough to ensure success?

Character in and of itself is not enough to be a great leader, but leaders do not become great without it. It is essential to be able to control how you respond to the uncontrollable events that happen to you and to do so in a positive manner.

Success Principle

"No leader will ever be without challenges for long. Character provides the inner resources that enable them to be overcome."

Lesson 21: Integrity has a Central Role

Critical to character is integrity. Leaders must hold themselves to higher standards that they expect of others. There is no other foundation so essential to success or worthy of your focus for development.

There is a widespread sense of lack of integrity at top levels, stimulated by the issue of executive pay, examples of customers' rights being abused for personal or corporate gain, and unethical behaviour uncovered by the press.

The need for improved standards of moral and ethical behaviour has become intense.

What does integrity really mean?

High integrity involves seeking total honesty, with yourself and others, by telling the truth and acting with complete congruence. It is inadequate to adopt the common approach of seeking to avoid the obvious lie while still using misleading, incomplete or inaccurate information.

People with integrity:

- Have nothing to hide or fear – they have the ground rules to allow them to make the essential choice between what they want to do and what they ought to do.

- Know that it is not possible to "talk the talk" without "walking the walk" consistently and in all areas of their life whilst also feeling good inside.

- Have learnt that their internal values have the most powerful influence on how they feel. They have developed a highly sensitive internal reference system to guide their choices and decisions based on high moral and ethical values.

- Do the right thing even when they know that no one will know whether they did so or not.

Integrity requires that you behave in an ethical way and do what you say you will do all the time – there is no room for flexibility.

How does lack of integrity by a leader impact employees?

It is really quite simple – if people feel that they cannot completely trust you in one area, they will find it very difficult to trust you at all.

It is a natural assumption (in other words, it generally happens below the level of conscious awareness) for people to infer that how you act in one instance will be carried over to others. This is why the revelation of a single indiscretion can have such a major impact. It can cast doubt over every accomplishment that a leader has achieved, no matter how honestly gained.

Does this mean you can never make a mistake?

Having integrity does not mean being right all of the time. I hope it is very clear to you after reading Lesson 18 that this is not possible for anyone – mistakes are inevitable.

All except the most intolerant and insecure people will forgive the occasional honest mistake, especially if they can see that your response to it is positive. What they find difficult to forgive are breaches of character or integrity that call your trustworthiness into question.

I suggest that your focus should be on your intention rather than the avoidance of mistakes. If you always approach every situation with the intention of acting for the greater good this will soon be widely recognised. You will gain trust and respect – and massively increase your influence in the process.

How will you benefit personally from greater integrity?

Lying is really a product of low self-esteem. It says that you don't believe that your abilities are great enough to get what you want in a positive way.

If you can shed the internal conflict created by a lack of integrity you will experience a huge sense of relief. You cannot be authentic if you pretend to be something you are not. By trying to do so you will live with the uncomfortable knowledge that your duplicity could be found out at any moment.

Any area where you are hiding things that you belief about yourself from others creates tension. It will be picked up by others as a lack of congruence and, more importantly, it suppresses your ability to fully express yourself.

Happiness researchers have found that one of the things that creates the greatest happiness is the internal sense of personal growth as we learn to express ourselves more fully. This has many times more impact on our happiness than any external factor arising from our conditions of living.

Developing greater integrity will allow you to grow in self-esteem and enable you to get more of what we ultimately all want most: to feel good.

Success Principle
"Immeasurable personal and professional benefits will be gained from developing higher integrity."

Lesson 22: Learn to Handle Rejection

All leaders will experience rejection and criticism by others. Their actions will be second guessed, broken apart, and analysed in the smallest detail. If they become senior enough, even people who have never met them will reject them.

In fact, rejection is a natural part of life. We were rejected: at school when we didn't get picked for the sports team or the part we wanted in the play, when we didn't get into the college of our choice, or when everyone forgot to invite us to the party. We will experience rejection if we don't get the job we apply for, if we get fired and if our spouse wants a divorce!

The problem is that most of us hate it so much that it ranks as one of the top fears that holds people back. If you are human you will experience fear of rejection to some degree. To be successful, particularly as a leader, you are going to have to learn how to handle it.

Why do people criticise?

As I mentioned earlier, criticising others requires little ability and is the approach taken by insecure people. The reason they do it stems from a belief that, "I am not enough" arising from the way the ego operates.

The primary mechanism of ego fulfilment is through comparison. To the ego it feels good to be doing better than others and to have more. Always more… Consequently it is constantly looking around at everyone else, judging what they do, what they have and even (maybe especially) what they look like. It will happily judge people harshly for nothing more than having different colour skin.

The world of the ego is controlled externally – dominated by the outcome of this judgement. This creates a real problem. If you live in the world of striving for the biggest yacht, fastest car, largest house or most expensive handbag, the problem is that there will always be someone who has a bigger one. Sooner or later you will inevitably feel inferior.

The easy option a critic has when things don't go their way is to seek faults in others to disguise their own. Rather than looking to the real cause of their feelings, which means staring their own insecurities in the face, they prefer the false sense of personal strength gained by focusing on the weakness of others.

Do people really feel better when they criticise?

People who criticise don't realise that their behaviours are purely an expression of their own limitations and self-doubts. Therefore they are always looking in the wrong direction for a solution.

The fulfilment to be gained from satisfying the ego is at best shallow and short-lived. This is particularly evident from investigating hormone activity in the body in certain situations. Studies have found that when we are kind to others we release endorphins, causing us to feel good. On the other hand, it can easily be demonstrated that our whole body goes weak if we even think about harming another person.

Overall, the person who suffers most from criticism is often the person giving it.

What is the best way to deal with the critics?

If you struggle with criticism, this stems from your interpretation of it – nothing is anything until we make it so through our interpretation (Lesson 7). Other people may criticise, but it requires our cooperation for us to feel rejected or to be otherwise troubled by it.

I find that remembering the following three points is usually enough to prevent me from taking critical comments to heart:

- Most people are not choosing their words. Their minds are in neutral and what they say is being driven by their conditioning. Rarely will they deliberately choose to hurt.

- The words that people use are really an expression of who they are, not of who I am. Kind people look for the good in others and critics don't know any better than to be led by their ego. It is not their fault, so I choose to feel compassion for them, knowing that they are suffering inside.

- The comments can be viewed as another form of feedback and that is how I seek to treat them – by seeing if there is anything to be learnt from them. Then moving on...

Egotism dictates that your abilities will rarely be unreservedly admired by those that don't have them. Don't allow the ego of others to hold you back from achieving what you are capable of.

Of even greater importance than handling the negative impact of others' egos is the ability to get your own ego out of the way. That is the subject of the next lesson.

Success Principle

"It is impossible to be successful as a leader while totally avoiding the criticism of others. Therefore, you must learn to be able to prevent what anyone else thinks from negatively affecting your mental state."

Lesson 23: Lead with Humility

In his outstanding book, *Good to Great*, Jim Collins provides powerful evidence of the value of humility. In his study of over 1,400 Fortune 500 companies he discovered that the very best leaders never sought personal recognition for their achievements.

By not having to stand out for the benefit of their ego, such leaders can maximise the ability of their team. The results of this approach speak for themselves. In allowing others to shine they engage the hearts of those that they lead, not just the heads.

Why is humility so rare then?

In the last lesson I addressed an aspect of how other people's ego can impact us. Of far greater importance to our own progress is our own ego and the limitations it creates.

I believe that most people are intuitively aware that the impact of the ego is detrimental to our efforts to achieve. This can be observed from the fact that to tell someone that they are egotistical is generally taken as a serious affront – a large ego is simply not something with which we want to be associated. It has immediate negative associations in our society which places high value on things like tolerance and openness.

The challenge for all of us is that the ego is present in everyone, to some degree. It is perfectly natural for us to want to feel that we have made the right choices. But the tendency that comes with it, to be judgemental, labelling things as right and wrong and condemning others for their behaviours, limits our ability to access humility.

How does your ego impact you personally?

Because of its need to win, the ego is full of fear, of the need for approval, of the need to control and of the need to manipulate. It is always judging based on previous experience and making choices based on the outcomes.

For example, most people meeting someone that they have not seen for some time but who previously insulted them would have great difficulty overlooking the previous injury. It would crop up automatically in their mind and create a barrier to communication. The other person would most likely get shut out.

Sensing this hostility, the other person would then naturally raise his defences, so both people would be hiding behind their own barricades. The initial moment of judgement caused by the repetition of old memories brought up the old grievances and ensured the repetition of the old experience as well. There can be no growth or development from that approach.

The greater the degree to which your ego provides your internal reference point, the more often you will experience grievances. Ego orientation turns life into a series of offences and perceived insults and creates a major barrier to the development of the quality of relationships that are needed as a leader.

How can humility be developed?

It is not possible to develop humility directly. What is needed instead is to constantly seek to let go of ego-based intentions. Much as the sun naturally shines once the clouds are removed, so your best self will automatically come through as your ego dissolves and you become more aware of your true potential. It cannot be forced to happen – you can only allow it to happen.

So a good starting point is the identification of ego-based behaviours. Examples that can help you become aware when your ego is at play are if you find yourself:

- Feeling offended or flattered.

- Seeking to win or being unwilling to accept or admit making a mistake.

- Being self-pitying or believing yourself to be a victim.

- Taking pleasure from being the best.

- Being preoccupied with yourself and what you claim as "yours".

- Experiencing Fear.

- Desiring recognition.

- Blaming others.

Through reflection and feedback it is possible to become progressively more aware of such behaviours. This self-awareness provides the key to change because it opens up the possibility of making more empowering choices.

Perhaps the most important such choice is to start seeing people as equals. In my experience it is a difficult concept for some people that being better AT something does not make them a better person. However, it is an incredibly powerful one to come to accept.

Through the process of this shift in perception you will recognise the great potential in everyone, including yourself. Humility follows as a natural consequence.

Paradoxically, as you become more aware of your own power and capability, you will also become more modest about your capabilities.

Success Principle

"Until you can get your ego out of the way you will severely limit your own potential as a leader."

Lesson 24: It's a People Business First

Many believe that business is about the provision of a product, a commodity, or a service. In reality every business is about people; those you lead and work with and those that supply you or buy your product. Without people there would be no business.

As we discussed in Lesson 15, every one of these people is driven by their own personal best interest. No one ever does anything because the business expects it. They will only deliver their best if what is required of them is in line with their own thinking and if what they do is appreciated.

Leaders must be able to inspire commitment in others and, in the process, create change by moving them toward new actions.

Surely we all do some things we don't want to do?

Yes, you can make someone do a job to a degree if there's fear involved. What is really happening in this case though, is that they will be choosing to do it because the alternative, as they perceive it, is worse. People will do a job that they hate because of what the loss of that job would mean to them, but ultimately they always have an option to walk away. While the pain threshold at which this option would be exercised will vary for different people, everyone would do so at some point.

This analysis, however, doesn't help all that much. What is much more important is the recognition that there is only one way that anyone will do a good job and that is IF THEY WANT TO. Ways must be found to encourage people to commit their discretionary effort if they are to perform at their best.

What this means is that if you are seeking to create real change at any level of the business (and you must if you want it to grow) each individual must be emotionally committed to be part of the change. That means you've got to find a way to motivate them that resonates with their personal goals; so they can see what's in it for them.

How can individual commitment be achieved?

To influence others to change it is first necessary to understand how they influence themselves. We must identify the thought processes that drive people to do what they do (or do not do), recognising that whatever they choose to engage in, they always do so for a reason.

Everyone is motivated by their own needs and expectations. One of the biggest mistakes many people make in seeking to influence others is to try to use the same strategy to motivate everyone they come across. There is no one-size-fits-all approach that works for motivation. We all have different needs and values, so it is essential that you seek to understand the most effective motivational approaches from the perspective of others.

To be successful you will need to relate to them and avoid the temptation to force them to do anything which they have not yet been convinced is a good idea. To do otherwise is not persuasion but intimidation and will never achieve the best long-term results.

What is the starting point?

As in a negotiation, the starting point in creating alignment and buy-in is to find out what others want. This is impossible while focusing only on what the business needs from them.

The goal is that they should adopt an idea as their own, then they will pursue it without continued motivation from you. Their own inspiration will carry them forward. Any time someone hasn't yet accepted your proposed solution, if you are able to reach an understanding of their individual interests and concerns then you have a much better chance of influencing them.

If you openly and willingly seek to find a win-win solution that allows you to give your employees what they want whilst also serving the needs of the business, you will create an environment in which everyone can be successful.

Success Principle

"To maximise your business every person needs to be fully motivated. If you treat everyone the same or tell them what they must do you will never earn their discretionary effort and they will not perform at their best."

Lesson 25: The Value of a Flexible Style

Flexibility is another vital trait of leaders. It refers to being adaptable to changes in circumstances so as to make the best of them. Creativity is essential in developing the flexibility necessary to optimise approach and to find empowering solutions for the daily issues and events that arise.

In relation to people, flexibility requires that you have a range of leadership styles at your disposal. With inadequate flexibility you will regularly meet people who you cannot influence effectively.

It follows then, that since influence is virtually synonymous with leadership, if you do not have flexibility, you are unlikely to be an effective leader.

Why is creativity important?

Creativity will free you to explore and experiment with different ways to improve your influence.

Neuro-Linguistic Programming (NLP) can be defined as the study of how to accelerate the achievement of excellence. One of its foundational principles suggests that in any human interaction the person with the most behavioural flexibility will ultimately determine the outcome.

This has significant implications to you as a leader when you are seeking to motivate new behaviours in someone else. Knowing that we all have a natural resistance to change (Lesson 11), it means that you must be able to find more ways to help them to change than they have of holding on to their old behaviour.

What happens when leaders are insufficiently flexible?

Even the simplest personality models have at least a dozen major types, so leaders must be proficient in using multiple styles if they are to be effective at reaching more than a small percentage of the audience.

Anyone who is incapable of sufficient flexibility will regularly find that themselves facing conflict situations – and may not realise that their own limitations are at the heart of them. While an accomplished leader would have found a way to create a win-win solution, the inflexible leader will need to fall back on force of character or position to get others to cooperate with his or her wishes.

The way that this normally shows itself in the workplace is that the leader becomes frustrated or angry. Having reached the end of their range of empowering behaviours they fall back on any other means that they are aware of to achieve their goals.

This is a trap for the unwary. In business, process matters. It is wrong to get other people to do what you want using physical force it must, therefore, also be wrong to do so using emotional force. The damage created by the emotional wake of doing so can massively outweigh the benefits gained.

The good news is that few people will adopt an aggressive approach if they are aware of how to achieve the same outcome in a more positive fashion. The solution, therefore, is to seek to improve awareness in this area.

What attitude works best?

As a leader, take the attitude that it is your job to make relationships work, not the other way around.

To be effective, you must take responsibility for the quality of your relationships, develop behavioural flexibility and adjust your approach to the needs of the person or group that you are dealing with. This means being competent in a range of styles and adopting the one that will be most effective in any given set of circumstances.

Where relationships break down, you empower yourself to repair them by accepting responsibility for the situation. You should never expect others to change so that you can remain the same. To do so is to require a higher level of leadership skill from others in this area than you are prepared to demonstrate yourself.

Success Principle

"Great flexibility is a fundamental requirement of outstanding leadership. Develop it consciously by being prepared to let go of your preferred style in favour of allowing others to keep theirs."

Lesson 26: Welcome Feedback

In Lesson 18 we discussed the importance of feedback. I explained how the recontextualization of what many people consider as "failure" changes its meaning and demonstrated feedback's critical role in the learning cycle.

Feedback is a vital element in raising our awareness of our current level of effectiveness. It is essential to be aware of how our behaviours impact others and where our results fall short of our desired outcomes. It is this that allows our approach to be amended and updated.

The best source of feedback is other people. It can also be obtained from personal observation and honest reflection, but the limitation of this approach is that it is difficult to see past our own blind spots.

What are the implications of poor feedback for leaders?

In the workplace, limited or poor feedback is most serious when it relates to the performance of a leader. Without it the leader will be isolated from the impact of poor decisions. This leads to future decisions becoming progressively less informed, which then damages credibility and further reinforces the isolation.

Where this cycle is most critical is among the poorest performing leaders. They have been found to have the largest gap between their own perception of their performance and how well they are actually doing. Their need for feedback is greatest, yet these are often the people who most resist it. In such cases it is very likely that their unwillingness to receive and act on feedback is actually at the root of their underperformance.

It is essential to become aware when your results fall short of your goals so that you can adjust your approach. That requires regular high quality feedback.

How well is feedback used in the workplace?

I'd like you to pause for a moment to answer these two questions as honestly as you can:

- Do you consider yourself to be good at giving feedback to others?

- Do you get as much high quality feedback as you would like?

I'm guessing that you probably answered "yes" to the first question and "no" to the second – overall, I estimate that over two thirds of people do. When I ask whole audiences these questions, as a general rule at least 80% answer yes to the first question and around 20% say no to the second.

This clearly highlights a systemic problem. Almost everyone wants more feedback but most of these same people must also be part of the problem because hardly anyone believes that they receive enough of it.

Why don't people like giving feedback?

People find it awkward and uncomfortable to give feedback for any of the following reasons:

- Fear of repercussions.

- Wanting to appear to be a great team player.

- Wanting to please the boss.

- A desire to be seen as being consistent with the division or company message.

- It feels uncomfortable because we don't want to hurt other people's feelings.

- Lack of knowledge of how to give feedback in a constructive way.

How do the best leaders respond?

The best leaders know the importance of feedback and actively seek it. So that the people they receive it from are not discouraged from giving further feedback in the future, they have also learnt to accept it in an open, friendly and non-defensive manner.

Receiving well is not enough on its own though, and they also know that how they change in response to the feedback is as important as how they behave in the moment. If someone has braved the fears and discomfort of providing feedback and you fail to demonstrate that you are prepared to take action on it, future feedback is likely to dry up very rapidly.

By demonstrating their willingness to learn through feedback leaders can make a significant contribution to the development of a learning organisation, the importance of which we will discuss in the next lesson.

Success Principle

"Without good feedback your personal development will be restricted and you will not have the information necessary to make good business decisions. You must actively encourage it, receive it openly and take action as a result."

Lesson 27: Organisations Must Learn Too

Failure to let go of the known is one of the major causes of stagnation in a company in exactly the same way as it is for an individual. To progress, a company must learn.

The challenge is that breaking an existing paradigm can be even harder for a whole organisation than it is for an individual – especially if the company is already successful. To maintain success it makes intuitive sense for them to seek to make everything they do perfectly replicable through the development of strong processes and systems.

The problem with this approach is that it leads to an excessive focus on the past. As IBM found out to its cost in the late 1980's and early 1990's, it does not work. It completely overlooks the factors that led to the success in the first place: the responsiveness to adapt and change, ability to learn and willingness to take risks.

Why is it so difficult for a company to change?

In many ways the behaviour of a company mirrors that of an individual:

- The part of the company that equates to the conscious mind is where people are aware of why things happen the way that they do. The many aspects that are measured and monitored, which operational managers and executives use as inputs to their decision-making processes, all fit into this region. So do processes, systems and corporate governance.

- The "subconscious" part of the company is its culture and norms. This is the element that determines whether the company will behave as a high-performing team or a loose collection of people working together to produce sub-optimal results.

Because of the difficulty of working with culture – as demonstrated by the low level of success of cultural change programmes – most leaders attempt to drive performance by managing what is going on at the conscious level. This will ultimately fail because, just as it is the subconscious beliefs of an individual that determine that person's results, sustained corporate results are the product of its culture and norms.

What is culture?

Most people readily talk about culture but few really understand its potential to insidiously undermine all efforts of leaders to improve corporate results. It exists as a shared set of beliefs and habits, and it is rarely well understood.

Culture determines how people think, act, and view the world around them. It is created naturally and automatically every time people come together with a shared purpose. Culture is powerful and invisible and its effects are far-reaching: it determines everything from a company's dress code to the work environment, to the rules for getting ahead and getting promoted.

In effect the culture of a business reflects the collective subconscious minds of everyone in the business. This is an area where leaders have no control, only influence, hence lending further importance to Lessons 19 to 21.

Where does learning come into this?

If you want to make significant, non-linear improvements to the effectiveness of your organisation then you must investigate its culture and work at the level of its paradigms and beliefs. This always means changing the minds of the people – and for people to change they must learn.

Learning does not happen automatically: it must be encouraged. Few people will take it on proactively without the support of the business and an environment in which it is comfortable for them to do so.

For the environment to stimulate growth leaders must recognise that when people do new things mistakes are inevitable (Lesson 18 – "Learn to Value Failure"). If they don't it will not be long before their staff seek instead to play it safe – to avoid losing what they have rather than trying to make things better. Playing it safe directly obstructs creativity and achievement. Under such circumstances no meaningful learning or progress is possible.

Success Principle

"To build a successful business leaders must address its culture, encouraging learning and minimising the stress that employees feel when they step outside their comfort zone."

Lesson 28: Total Accountability

Leaders who are not prepared to take responsibility, to be held accountable for their team or area, will never perform well – in all likelihood they'll fail. They are too afraid of stepping out and of making the tough decisions, and waste their time seeking to ensure that they always have someone to point the finger at when things go wrong.

Anyone exhibiting these behaviours clearly doesn't believe in their ability to create the outcomes that they want or to recover effectively from setbacks. This lack of self-confidence prevents effective functioning as a leader.

People who won't take responsibility will rarely create anything of significance.

How does taking responsibility change things?

Avoiding responsibility is a clear indication that the mind has made a decision: that the situation in question is beyond its ability to sufficiently control or influence in order to guarantee the desired results. Once caught in this mindset the person concerned loses access to a huge proportion of their capability – becoming powerless.

By saying, "I am responsible for this" a very clear instruction is given to the subconscious mind that it must start to look for a solution. As we discussed in Lesson 5, powerlessness arises simply from a lack of awareness about how to deal with the situation at hand. Even the beginnings of a solution start to give a person back their internal power.

Personal power is an inner awareness that helps us to feel in control of our lives. It is an inner knowing that we can achieve our goals, a calm conviction about who we are and our ability to get the things we want in life. It is released and magnified by taking full responsibility for our own actions. It is also a key component of self-leadership.

To be an effective leader in business, however, personal responsibility is not enough. It is also necessary to take responsibility for the performance of a team. By doing so, leaders similarly give themselves permission to find ways to overcome the problems facing the team.

What attitude would this type of leader have?

A measure of how a leader accepts responsibility and accountability is the way that he or she deals with success and failure. We have all seen leaders who love to take the credit when things go well but who quickly blame others when performance slips. This is not the behaviour of an effective leader.

If you want to be an effective leader you must seek to give credit to your employees when things go well. Never take personal credit for things completed by others or the team. This approach will create the best and most enduring returns for your business. At the same time you must understand the need to shield your team when things go wrong.

By taking responsibility for errors and mistakes and seeking to identify what you might have done better, you prevent the creative spirit of the team from being undermined. Your employees already know who is or isn't at fault without it being revealed to the world. Their response to having been shielded in this way will most likely be to seek to prove themselves worthy of this treatment.

What do "responsible" behaviours look like?

The behaviours associated with feelings of responsibility depend on who you are dealing with and fall into one of 3 categories:

- With your team: Demonstrate that you are the leader by never avoiding the tough decisions. Set individual goals and delegate the responsibility for achieving them. In circumstances of poor performance by some members of the team, act to protect the best interests of the team as a whole while still valuing all concerned as human beings.

- With more senior management: Accept responsibility for mistakes. Use tenacity and persistence to ensure that their expectations are fully met. Push them to make timely and necessary decisions even where there might be a personal risk in doing so. Also, champion your team to them, taking opportunities to allow your staff direct exposure to them.

- With other areas in the business: Ensure that when jobs need doing they get done. Even if there is no immediate reward, get things done if it is the right thing for the organisation as a whole. Use resources as though they were your own.

Success Principle

"The willingness to be held fully accountable for the performance of other people and a focus on achievement rather than recognition are essential hallmarks of effective leadership."

Lesson 29: Develop Strengths

There are many attributes, competencies and skills that contribute to leadership but becoming great does not require development of them all. Research shows that people with strength in only a few areas usually become great leaders.

If you want to grow leadership capability, the fastest way to do it is to concentrate on the areas that can be made into stand-out-from-the-crowd strengths most easily – in other words, those where you or others you work with are already strongest.

What is wrong with focusing on weaknesses?

To focus on weaknesses is a very common strategy. Presented with an assessment of their leadership competencies most people are drawn to focus on the least positive items. The reasoning seems to be that their level of performance is determined by the weakest areas.

I believe this is the result of conditioning by our education system, where the emphasis is on improvement through focusing on what is wrong. To get from 60% to 70% you had to fix your errors. To get into your university of choice you had to avoid any of your exam grades slipping below the required level, no matter how great your strengths were. It may also be that we just inherently dislike being seen to be weak at anything – this is just the ego at work again (Lessons 22 & 23).

Either way, carrying forward this approach into work, people first seek to tackle their greatest weaknesses and once they have been addressed (if they are successful, which as you will see below is not assured) they move onto the next weakest area, and so on. Over time they end up with a nice consistent profile with no major weaknesses (or strengths).

There are two major problems with this approach:

- A consistently average profile with no weaknesses still produces below average results.

- Weaknesses usually develop in areas that people either don't enjoy or in which they have limited natural ability, or both. Either way, asking anyone to do more in such areas is likely to be demotivating and will rarely bring out their best.

Don't weaknesses sometimes totally undermine a leader?

Definitely. A weakness that is significantly lower than the other areas needs to be handled differently.

Such a weakness may be considered to be a fatal flaw. If it is not corrected it will have an extremely negative effect and drag down the overall perception of leadership effectiveness, particularly if it is in one of these 5 areas:

- Inability to learn from mistakes (Lesson 18).

- Lack of interpersonal skills (Lessons 4 to 6, and generally throughout the book).

- Lack of openness to new ideas (Lessons 11, 25 & 26).

- Failure to take personal responsibility for the performance of a work group (Lesson 28).

- Lack of action (Introduction and throughout the book).

One thing that is obvious about all of these areas is that they are emotional and behavioural – not intellectual. What is needed to address them is high quality feedback, preferably by a skilled coach or mentor because of the objectivity they can bring to the process.

How can development be maximised?

The impact of focusing on further developing strengths rather than removing weaknesses is profound. While pulling all competencies up to an average level still results in below average results, if instead one area can be made into a strength that stands out, overall performance is immediately likely to rise to well above average.

Extending this approach, research shows that if a leader can develop just 4-6 competencies into strengths their overall performance is likely to be outstanding. This is something that can be applied throughout an organisation to create leaders from top to bottom.

Success Principle

"No one ever became great by aiming for the "middle ground." Greatness requires stand-out competencies developed by focusing on positive areas and making them even stronger. It requires that we build on strengths."

Lesson 30: Collaboration Really Works

One of the most difficult challenges for you as a leader is how to get the most out of your team. Even if you have lots of great people, that will usually not be enough on its own. There are many teams full of talented individuals that do not realise their full potential. Great individual performances are of little significance if the team does not win.

Teamwork is always at the heart of high performance. It is surprising, then, that a high level of teamwork is so rarely found in today's workplace, particularly at the senior levels of an organisation.

How does a team become successful?

There are many models available that describe the development stages of teams. One model that I like for its effectiveness and simplicity describes team development as progressing through 3 levels:

- Level 1, **Inclusion**. This occurs primarily when a team is created. The members of the team typically feel isolated and have a strong drive to be accepted. They will often compromise their own ideals and conform to the views of others in order to meet their emotional needs. No one performs at their best.

- Level 2, **Assertion**. This is achieved once the majority of members of the team feel included. The informal hierarchy of the team becomes established and the driving force of the team is internal competition. There will regularly be examples of high productivity from some team members, but usually at the expense of others. The team lacks cohesion.

- Level 3, **Cooperation**. Real creativity becomes possible. The energy of the team is directed towards common goals and members are highly supportive of each other. Dynamic tension is retained but does not destabilise because of the attitude and trust established within the team.

Despite the obvious evidence of the success of cooperation in many other fields of endeavour, the type of genuine cooperation seen at Level 3 is very unusual in business. This represents a major opportunity for businesses that want to get ahead.

Doesn't the heat of competition create the ultimate results?

I regularly get challenged over the view that collaboration produces the best results by people using sport as an example. After all, the argument goes, at the highest levels of achievement isn't it the best competitors that win?

While I understand the reasoning behind this belief, there are two fundamental points which provide important evidence why competition does not really deliver the results it might initially seem to do:

1. While a champion may be crowned as a result of winning a competition, the thing that got them there was a clear

focus on their goal and many hours of practice to develop the skills, speed, strength and stamina required (Lesson 12). They never achieve the levels necessary from competition alone. Also, during their practice time the people that they work with seek to help them, not compete with them.

2. Much of the practice of a champion is specifically aimed at being able to develop the mental attributes necessary to win. They must be able to remain calm on demand and in the face of enormous pressure. There are lots of people with great skills who cannot master competition because they haven't enough emotional mastery. Even at the highest levels of performance, competition diminishes achievement for anyone who does not have the mental toughness to exclude the effects of the competition from their thinking. Observe any world-class sportsman or woman and this is totally evident.

People who become the best do so despite the competition, not because of it.

Can cooperation really work in business?

For many, collaboration is not a realistic expectation in business, probably because they have an intuitive understanding of the difficulty of taming individual egos on the team. Unless cooperation is essential to even remain in the game, it may seem unlikely that competitiveness in the team can be tamed.

This view accurately reflects the likelihood that the task will not be easy. The competitiveness of the ego is hard to overcome.

Success is most likely if the change is led from the top. Everyone must know how they are expected to contribute to the overall team and reward structures must be aligned with the new behaviours that are sought.

The culture of the team must also be right. A climate must be fostered that stimulates creativity, is tolerant of mistakes, and in which everyone feels valued.

Success Principle

"The achievement of interdependence and cooperation in a team is an outcome of true leadership. Realising it is not easy but the benefit to be gained is a transformation of the performance of your business."

Lesson 31: Leadership is Not a Position

Leadership requires a certain attitude of mind. It entails a willingness to be courageous, to be prepared to be different, to go first, to risk rejection and to seek to influence change. None of these things are a function of title or position. They are a choice.

Leadership is a choice (Lesson 3).

Hierarchical command and control models that were common in the past did allow people to exercise leverage over others by virtue of their position, but this use of force wasn't real leadership. Recently, the greater importance of trust and influence versus position power and structure has become increasingly evident – as the knowledge economy gains further strength we can expect to see this trend continuing.

As this happens, those that have relied upon position power to get things done will be increasingly marginalised and become even less effective.

What will replace position power?

The type of leadership that is now becoming increasingly prevalent is not actually new at all. It combines the determination to be the best that one can be with an attitude of service. It is characterised by a mindset of seeking to give more than one receives.

Such leadership cannot be awarded or dictated and is the sort of leadership demonstrated by Mahatma Gandhi. He had no army, never held or accepted political office, never used violence, and had no status symbols or trappings of power at all. He was a small, frail man, yet he defeated the armed might of the British Empire, driving the British out of India without firing a single shot.

The key to Gandhi's power was his incredible influence over the hearts and minds of the people of India. Through the power of his own conviction he was able to align 300 million people behind a single objective and to ensure that they sought to achieving it without resorting to violence. A leadership feat with few parallels.

What Gandhi demonstrated is that real power is never about overpowering others but is instead the act of acknowledging and encouraging their power. Nothing he did was about personal gain. He modelled humility and showed that authentic leadership is not about the desire for followers or having people serving you.

If the current trend continues, with more and more people connecting to the deeper motivators of their behaviour, particularly their desire to grow and contribute to others, this type of leadership will become much more prevalent. Because it creates improved results, people who operate from this mindset will naturally rise to the top.

When is the best time for you to start?

The highest performers never wait for their conditions to change before making a start. In the search for personal advancement they know that the timing will never be just right and don't they shy away from the difficult task of personal change.

You will only reach your potential tomorrow by dedicating yourself to growth today. The more effort that you are prepared to put into this area, getting expert help if necessary, the greater your ability to realise what your potential will be.

To be successful you must be prepared to sacrifice who you are now for who you can become. Most people don't understand sacrifice, thinking that they will have to suffer in some way, but that is not what it is about at all. What it really means is to give up something of lesser value to get something greater. This is essential to growth.

The willingness and capacity to continue to improve your skills is one of the most important aspects of leadership. As you learn to let go of inhibiting beliefs and habits you will unleash more of your potential. You will have the opportunity to become a true leader, able to lead yourself and others.

It is your responsibility as a leader to do this – to make the most of yourself so that you become an inspirational role model for others to help them to do the same.

What enables this to happen?

Everything starts with the way that you think.

Of primary importance is your ability to change the way that you think when faced with new challenges – to open your mind to new possibilities. Each time you choose to stop and think, rather than allowing your instant reaction to dominate your activity, you create the opportunity for a breakthrough that changes another aspect of your conditioning.

The quality of our lives is not dictated by what happens to us but by how we respond to what happens to us. This book has been set in the context of the business environment, but the ability to respond rather than react has a far more wide-ranging impact than that. It will enable you to improve almost any aspect of your life. I encourage you to develop your capacity to use it.

Success Principle

"The only way to get ahead and stay ahead is to dedicate yourself to growth today. If you have a team you must also provide opportunities for them to do the same."

Staying on the Journey

I hope that this book has inspired you to think more deeply about leadership and that it may have helped to create a greater commitment to the ongoing development of your own skills. This is the most assured route to improving your results.

All advancement in the world may be attributed to a leader of some description – people who are prepared to go out and create something new, to make a difference. Through my company, Optimal Track Ltd, I am committed to helping as many people as possible to transform their results through leadership.

To find out about the full range of services and tools for personal growth that I can offer please visit my web sites:

www.michaelnicholas.com

www.optimaltrack.com

Here you will find a range of resources including personal coaching, in-person and online seminars, online courses and training programmes for you and your team.

Alternatively, simply contact me or one of my team to arrange an informal telephone conversation.

Telephone: 0844 736 5678

E-mail: contactus@optimaltrack.com

Thank you, Michael Nicholas

Also by Michael Nicholas:
Being The Effective Leader

Leadership is an Inside-out Process. Consequently, only by internal change can we increase external influence.

It's going to take a new kind of leader to succeed in today's testing environment – and the challenge to be faced is not efficiency but effectiveness. Radical changes in world markets and the workplace are demanding greatly refined influencing skills.

The compelling question in this environment is: "Can anyone become an outstanding leader and, if so, how?" *Being The Effective Leader* provides the answer, revealing the underlying attributes required for success. Delving far beyond what leaders are required to do, it explores the core issue of how they must be. If you are seeking world class results, it persuasively demonstrates that it is essential to become the type of leader that others will eagerly follow.

Being The Effective Leader is your handbook to enable you to not only become more effective but also to gain more fulfilment in the process. It will show you how to transform our relationships with others and become that most effective of leaders: someone who creates leaders around you.

Praise for *Being The Effective Leader*:

"A great book, an important book for it convincingly states the crucial fact that true leadership comes from inside ourselves, if we have the courage to look; not from business schools – or books, except for this one."

~ **Sir John Whitmore**, author of *Coaching for Performance*

"If you want to make a change in your life, *Being The Effective Leader* will make a difference in your approach and give you information that will not only show you how to change, but will also inspire you to do so."

~ **Jim Sloane**, Vice Chairman, Deloitte & Touche UK

"I found *Being The Effective Leader* to be a must read for anyone who leads others. Not only does it explain why we are getting our current results, it offers sound business advice about how to improve them."

~ **Peter Thomson**, One of the UK's Leading Strategists On Business and Personal Growth

"This detailed and rigorous exploration of the impact of thinking processes and beliefs on leadership is very much overdue. Michael Nicholas uncovers the habits of thinking and behaviours that will enable you to become a world class leader."

~ **Steve Siebold**, author of *177 Mental Toughness Secrets of the World Class*

Available from: **www.BeingTheEffectiveLeader.com**.

About Michael Nicholas

Michael Nicholas is an author, coach, corporate trainer and professional speaker. He is the Managing Director of Optimal Track Ltd., an organisation offering coaching and training for leaders and teams from medium size businesses to leading FTSE companies.

Michael did not start out as a coach. After graduating from Durham University and serving seven years as a commissioned officer in the Royal Air Force, he left the service as a chartered electrical engineer. Subsequently he gained broad and extensive experience in the business world, including running a pan-European professional services division and as a director in the strategy practice at Deloitte Consulting.

As his career progressed, he became increasingly involved in and absorbed by leadership coaching. He attended both business-sponsored and voluntary training courses and applied the lessons he learnt to his day-to-day tasks and interactions with his team and colleagues. Ultimately this led to him founding Optimal Track in 2004. Since then, in additional to his work with organisations, he has also trained several hundred people globally to become effective coaches.

All Michael's work is built around one central philosophy: that everybody has far more potential than they realise. He is committed to helping people to rapidly unleash their potential, thereby radically transforming their results. All his programmes are completely customised around the needs of his clients and, by working at the level of the root causes of human behaviour, results are achieved that are sustainable after they return to their desks.